CODE NAME PAULINE

MEMOIRS OF A WORLD WAR II SPECIAL AGENT

Pearl Witherington Cornioley
with Hervé Larroque

Edited by Kathryn J. Atwood

CHICAGO REVIEW PRESS

The Library of Congress has cataloged the hardcover edition as follows:
Cornioley, Pearl Witherington, 1914-2008.
Code name Pauline: memoirs of a World War II special agent / Pearl Witherington
Cornioley with Hervé Larroque; edited by Kathryn J. Atwood.
pages cm.—(Women of action)
Summary: "Pearl Witherington Cornioley, one of the most celebrated female World
War II resistance fighters, shares her remarkable story in this firsthand account of her
experience as a special agent for the British Special Operations Executive (SOE). Told
through a series of reminiscences—from a difficult childhood spent in the shadow of
World War I and her family's harrowing escape from France as the Germans approached
in 1940 to her recruitment and training as a special agent and the logistics of parachuting
into a remote rural area of occupied France and hiding in a wheat field from enemy fire—
each chapter also includes helpful opening remarks to provide context and background
on the SOE and the French Resistance. With an annotated list of key figures, an appendix
of original unedited interview extracts—including Pearl's fiance; Henri's story—and
fascinating photographs and documents from Pearl's personal collection, this memoir will
captivate World War II buffs of any age"—Provided by publisher.
  Summary: "The as yet unpublished memoirs for young adults of the only female SOE
agent to lead a French Resistance network during World War II "—Provided by publisher.
  Includes bibliographical references and index.
  ISBN 978-1-61374-487-1 (hardback)
  1. Cornioley, Pearl Witherington, 1914–2008. 2. World War, 1939–1945—Underground
movements—France—Juvenile literature. 3. World War, 1939–1945—Secret service—
Great Britain—Juvenile literature. I. Larroque, Hervé. II. Atwood, Kathryn J., editor. III.
Title.

D802.F8C626 2013
940.54'8641092—dc23
[B]
                                        2013008734

Cover and interior design: Sarah Olson
Except where otherwise noted, all interior photos courtesy of Hervé Larroque / Éditions
  par exemple with permission of Pearl Witherington Cornioley.
Front cover images (from top): Background map by istockphoto; Pearl Witherington,
  September 18, 1944, in Levroux, France; and image from Pearl Witherington's false
  railway pass, courtesy of Hervé Larroque.

Printed in the United States of America
5 4 3 2 1

CODE NAME PAULINE

OTHER BOOKS IN THE
WOMEN OF ACTION SERIES

*Double Victory: How African American Women Broke Race
and Gender Barriers to Help Win World War II*

The Many Faces of Josephine Baker: Dancer, Singer, Activist, Spy

*Reporting Under Fire: 16 Daring Women War
Correspondents and Photojournalists*

*Women Aviators: 26 Stories of Pioneer Flights,
Daring Missions, and Record-Setting Journeys*

*Women Heroes of the American Revolution: 20 Stories of
Espionage, Sabotage, Defiance, and Rescue*

*Women Heroes of World War I: 16 Remarkable
Resisters, Soldiers, Spies, and Medics*

*Women Heroes of World War II: 26 Stories of
Espionage, Sabotage, Resistance, and Rescue*

*Women in Space: 23 Stories of First Flights, Scientific
Missions, and Gravity-Breaking Adventures*

*Women of Steel and Stone: 22 Inspirational Architects,
Engineers, and Landscape Designers*

*Women of the Frontier: 16 Tales of Trailblazing
Homesteaders, Entrepreneurs, and Rabble-Rousers*

*A World of Her Own: 24 Amazing Women
Explorers and Adventurers*

To productive international relationships, represented most dramatically by the French section of the British Special Operations Executive during World War II; later by the willingness of an initially reluctant British subject, Pearl Cornioley, to be interviewed by Hervé Larroque, a French journalist; and finally, by the friendship between M. Larroque and John Atwood, an American, initiated by their shared respect for Pearl Witherington, continued because of their mutual willingness to communicate in the other's language, and without which this edition of Pearl Witherington's memoir would not have been possible.

— • —

I don't like blowing my own trumpet. I find it really difficult, but at the same time I want people to know what really happened.

—PEARL WITHERINGTON CORNIOLEY

— • —

CONTENTS

EDITOR'S NOTE

BY KATHRYN J. ATWOOD

What you hold in your hand is not a history book. It is a piece of history. History books are often written by people who were not there. This is the testimony of someone who not only was there but who actively participated in what happened. It is what historians call "original source material."

Pearl Witherington was an agent of the Special Operations Executive (SOE), a British wartime organization that secretly trained and sent agents into Nazi-occupied countries during World War II. Immediately following the war, the British public was shocked to learn that female agents had worked behind enemy lines for the SOE, risking their lives and in some instances losing them, in the fight against the Nazis. Books were written and films produced about these women for a fascinated public who couldn't seem to get enough. Pearl became very distrustful of such endeavors after an author wrote a book that fictionalized her wartime work to make it seem more dramatic than it had been. When the stories of other agents were deliberately altered in similar ways in books and films, Pearl refused to give any interviews for many years.

Toward the end of her life, however, she began to feel that her story might be inspiring to young people in difficult circumstances. French journalist Hervé Larroque approached her in 1994 with the idea of writing her memoir, and as their acquaintance progressed she felt she could trust him to handle her story properly. He conducted multiple interviews, some with Pearl alone and others including Pearl's husband, Henri Cornioley, from December 1994 through June 1995. The transcript of those interviews was published in French by Éditions par exemple in December 1995, with the title *Pauline*, one of Pearl's wartime code names.

M. Larroque appreciated what I had done with Pearl's story in my book *Women Heroes of World War II*, in which she is profiled, and agreed to have me edit the English translation of *Pauline* into a straight narrative with added introductory material to place the memoir within its historical context.

Because Pearl was adamant that her story not be altered, I have taken great care to change as little of her own wording as possible. In most instances, M. Larroque's brief questions are simply incorporated into the text. A large part of the editing process involved bringing together material on one subject that had been garnered from various interviews and was found in various sections of the manuscript. What remains is Pearl's story in her own choice of words and her own style of speaking.

Because Pearl's husband, Henri, was present during some of the interviews, there is specific material—enlightening comments by Henri, humorous interchanges between him and Pearl—that would be lost if converted into a narrative. There are other sections where keeping the text in its original dialogue format provides more clarity. A selection of these can be found in the appendix.

I am very honored to present Pearl Witherington's memoir to the English-reading public at last. May the memory of her courage and determination in the face of great difficulty continue to inspire future generations.

PREFACE

BY HERVÉ LARROQUE

This book is intended primarily for young adults. It relates the authentic story of "Pauline," Pearl Witherington, who enlisted in 1943 in a secret British service—the SOE(F)—to help the resistance in France. After several months of intensive training, she "parachuted in" the night of September 22–23, 1943. She was 29 years old.

After that, she lived an unusual life for seven months. Most of the time, traveling on night trains, she went to deliver messages, the content of which she rarely understood. She accompanied people as a guide, transported materials, and communicated back to London via coded radio messages. She was what was called a "courier."

This work, done in solitary fashion, was obviously dangerous, for she could have been arrested and exposed at any moment by the Gestapo or by the French police. She had several occasions to be quite afraid! *Pauline* recounts her life at that time, put up here and there at the homes of trustworthy friends and disguised with a false identity: Marie Verges, cosmetics representative.

In May 1944 the head of her network was taken by the Germans: she changed her location and her mode of life. She found shelter in the guardhouse of an estate in the Cher River valley in central France, where she organized a small resistance group with Henri Cornioley, her fiancé. On June 11, 1944, they were very nearly taken and killed by the Germans. In a few weeks, the resistance group grew, then was divided into four subgroups. By July 1944, they had 1,500 effectives. Their leader, whom very few knew personally, was called Pauline.

For Pearl and Henri, the war ended that September. They went to England and turned over all the money that remained from the parachute drops—to the great astonishment of the military administration, who had never seen such a thing. A few weeks later they were married, in great simplicity. They had no money, nor any employment.

In this book, Pearl, with Henri's help on occasion, recounts the good times, the diverse aspects, the amazing or funny stories of her life during the five years of the war. She also recounts her youth, not at all rosy: four little English girls living in Paris with their mother, without work and speaking French poorly, while their father traveled the world and forgot to pay the rent. The one who made up for the deficiencies of the absent father was Pearl. It was she who went to the market to salvage half-rotten potatoes for the family to eat. But she talks about these things without anger or bitterness. "I have no resentment against life for giving me this difficult childhood," she confides, "given that it gave me the strength to fight the rest of my life."

Pearl had an open character, curious about things and people. Lucky for us, she had the memory of an elephant.

This book is also the history of a couple. For Pearl and Henri, that history was strewn with obstacles. Their families prevented them from seeing each other, the war separated them for several years, and liberation found them without resource or home. After 10 years of struggles, of patience, and of joys, life finally allowed them to be together. They celebrated their 50-year wedding anniversary in 1994. What were their ages, in fact, at the time of my interviews? Pearl was 80 and Henri 84. Their stories prove that age remains, above all, a matter of the soul and the heart. Henri and Pearl were not sour or sad or withdrawn into themselves. Quite the contrary.

This text makes no pretense to being elegant literature: it is a real testimony told with everyday words. My main guideline when transcribing notes and tape recordings was respect for the facts: there was no thought of romanticizing anything.

Pearl and Henri didn't agree about everything, but they held in common some important traits, traits you could call altruism, courage, and youthfulness. Their story can be, no doubt, a source of hope and strength to young people who are confronted with a challenging life.

Up until the time of my interviews, Pearl had refused to expose her personal history in such a manner—it was only for its potential benefit to young people that she eventually agreed to do so.

INTRODUCTION

On October 21, 1940, when the Blitz—the German bombing of British cities—was in full swing, Winston Churchill gave the following speech over BBC (British Broadcasting Corporation) radio to any people in Nazi-occupied France who might be listening:

> Frenchmen! For more than 30 years, in peace and war, I marched with you and I am marching still along the same road. Tonight I speak to you at your firesides wherever you may be, or whatever your fortunes are. . . . Here at home in England, under the fire of the Boche, we do not forget the ties and links that unite us to France . . .
>
> Here in London, which Herr Hitler says he will reduce to ashes and which his airplanes are now bombarding, our people are bearing up unflinchingly. Our air force has more than held its own. We are waiting for the long-promised invasion. So are the fishes.
>
> Remember we shall never stop, never weary, and never give in, and that our whole people and empire have

vowed themselves to the task of cleansing Europe from the Nazi pestilence and saving the world from the new Dark Ages. Do not imagine, as the German-controlled wireless tells you, that we English seek to take your ships and colonies. We seek to beat the life and soul out of Hitler and Hitlerism—that alone, that all the time, that to the end . . .

Good night, then: sleep to gather strength for the morning. For the morning will come. Brightly will it shine on the brave and true, kindly upon all who suffer for the cause, glorious upon the tombs of heroes. Thus will shine the dawn.

Vive la France!

It was necessary for the British prime minster to remind the French of their countries' mutual ties: a few months earlier, beginning on May 26, 1940, the British Expeditionary Force (BEF)—trained British soldiers who had come to assist France against the German invasion during the Battle of France—evacuated for Great Britain via the shores of Dunkirk, leaving France to fight Germany alone. Although the BEF, much smaller than the French army, had been overwhelmed by the Germans, many French people felt betrayed by Operation Dynamo, the British evacuation from Dunkirk. They felt even more betrayed when, shortly after the French had surrendered to the Germans on June 22, 1940, the British sunk a powerful fleet of French ships near Algeria after the French navy refused to surrender them—killing more than 1,000 sailors in the process—in order to prevent Germany from using the ships to invade Britain.

France and Britain had been allies—if somewhat mistrustful ones—during World War I and had simultaneously declared war on Germany when the Nazis had invaded Poland on September

1, 1939. But by the time Churchill delivered his encouraging speech, many of the French saw Britain as a traitor, and because most of Europe lay in the shadow of the swastika, Churchill's words of hope seemed empty. However, at that moment, the British prime minister was preparing to offer those in Nazi-occupied countries more than just words: he had already given the go-ahead to an organization that would help them fight their Nazi oppressors.

A few months earlier, on July 16, 1940, when the Battle of Britain—the air war between the German Luftwaffe and Britain's Royal Air Force (RAF)—had begun in the skies above Britain, Hitler had issued an official directive called Operation Sea Lion, ordering the invasion of Great Britain. That same night, Winston Churchill summoned his minister of economic warfare, Hugh Dalton, and famously directed him to "set Europe ablaze" with an organization, initially planned by the government of the previous prime minister, Neville Chamberlain, that would locate, assist, supply, and train willing resisters within occupied countries by sending them British-trained agents who were native speakers of the occupied country, or who could pass as such. The organization was to be top secret, and it wasn't until years later that most people discovered its name: the Special Operations Executive (SOE).

However, those within the British Secret Intelligence Service (MI6 or SIS) found out about it almost immediately and were very critical of the new organization. They were afraid that the SOE's main objectives—sabotage of the German war machine—would adversely affect MI6's quiet gathering of information. And because the need to fight the Nazis from within the occupied countries was urgent, SOE agents trained for a relatively short period of time, causing MI6 to brand it unprofessional and amateurish, an opinion that was initially shared by the other branches of the armed services. This was a problem, especially at first, because the SOE would have to depend on the other branches for supplies and transportation.

Referred to during the war as the Inter-Services Research Bureau, the SOE was headquartered at 64 Baker Street in London, near the address of the fictional detective Sherlock Holmes, and the SOE agents were sometimes referred to as the Baker Street Specials or the Baker Street Irregulars, named after some street children employed by Holmes to secretly ferret out information. That nickname called attention to the irregular type of warfare SOE agents would collectively engage in; that is, warfare generally conducted outside the activities of the regular armed forces—the destruction of munitions factories and communication lines, guerilla warfare, assassination, and harming the morale of the enemy—anything that would disrupt and hinder the German war machine occupying much of mainland Europe.

The SOE had different sections named for the country that particular section was supporting. The largest section—the one that eventually contained the largest number of SOE agents— was the French, or F Section: any Allied invasion of Nazi-occupied Europe would necessarily begin with France, just across the channel from Great Britain. After its surrender to Germany, France had been divided into two zones: the northern and western "occupied zone" (where the Germans were more visibly in charge) and the southern "free zone." The free zone was controlled by a puppet government of Nazi Germany under Marshal Pétain, the beloved French military hero from World War I. His headquarters were in the town of Vichy, and so the southern region was referred to as Vichy France during the war.

Resistance was slow to begin in France, especially in the southern section, where initially the Germans were not as

visible and so the reality of occupation not as noticeable as it was
in the north. But resistance to the occupying Germans *and* to
the Vichy government grew when they instituted, first, a trade-
off of French POWs for French workers to toil in German munitions factories and, second, the Service du Travail Obligatoire
(STO), a subsequent and increasing demand for an enormous
number of French factory workers to be sent to Germany. The
result was large groups of young men fleeing into rural areas
and forming into bands eager to fight the Germans. They were
called Maquis, named after a dense plant formation that grew
wild on the French island of Corsica. Many of these groups were
eventually recruited, organized, supplied, armed, and trained
by the SOE.

French politics were severely divided before the war, and the
resistance groups that formed—including the Maquis—during
the occupation reflected those divisions. The armed branch of
French Communists was called the Francs-Tireurs et Partisans
(Free Fighters and Partisans), or the FTP. At first, French Communists weren't terribly interested in resisting the German
occupation, as they saw the war as a conflict between imperi-
alistic countries. But after Germany declared war on the Soviet
Union, the Communist-based Maquis groups became very eager
to fight the Germans.

On the other end of the political spectrum was the Armée
Secrète, the AS, which was composed largely of former members of the defeated French army who were loyal to General
Charles de Gaulle, a French military leader who had been
opposed to the armistice (the official surrender) with Germany
and who eventually became an inspiring figure to many French
people during the occupation. General de Gaulle broadcast
radio messages of resistance from his headquarters in London,
where he also led a fighting force called the French Forces of

the Interior (FFI) along with his own section of the SOE called the RF Section. The RF agents were nearly all French citizens, and this section was created by the SOE specifically to answer to de Gaulle's headquarters. (De Gaulle went so far as to insist that the SOE not recruit any native French men or women into the SOE F Section, and while this was not followed consistently, the SOE did attempt to avoid the RF Section in France as much as possible.)

Although there were serious attempts to unify the various strands of the French Resistance, the political situation remained somewhat complex throughout the war. It was into this complicated state of affairs that the first F Section agent of the SOE was parachuted into central France on the night of May 5–6, 1941. In the end, more than 400 SOE agents were sent into France during the course of the occupation, and 39 of them were women.

Pearl Witherington was one of these women. Although the SOE trained her to be a courier for a Resistance circuit called the Stationer network, nothing but her own strength, intelligence, and determination could have prepared her for the drastic change in roles that occurred while she was working in occupied France, a change that has made her one of the most celebrated female agents in SOE history.

CODE NAME PAULINE

PROLOGUE

One day a German asked me, "Why did you do it; what pushed you to become involved in the resistance?" I said, "Intense anger," and it was true. Intense anger against all the injustices.

We could see the bombing in London and we heard of the battles going on in Africa and other places. But what made me really furious was the occupation. When I arrived in Paris from Normandy, shortly after July 14, 1940, notices were placarded, "Mr. So and So was shot last night." There were notices like that on columns along rue de Rivoli. Those poor people had been caught outside after the curfew, taken to a police station, and if there was any action whatsoever against the Germans during the night, they were shot. That is what a hostage is: some poor defenseless person. And that is something I cannot abide.

Imagine that someone comes into your home—someone you don't like—he settles down, gives orders: "Here we are, we're at home now; you must obey." To me that was unbearable.

3

1

A DIFFICULT CHILDHOOD

Pearl Witherington's father, Wallace Witherington, was the last male descendant of an ancient British warrior family, the most famous member being Sir Richard Witherington, who legend tells had both his feet cut off during the battle of Otterburn in 1388 yet continued to fight on his knees. Despite this impressive lineage, Pearl's father was an alcoholic, and this caused tremendous difficulty for his family.

Both of Pearl's parents were British citizens who were living in France when their children were born. Their oldest child, Cécile Pearl, was born in Paris on June 24, 1914, just months before the start of World War I. Pearl remained a British citizen for the rest of her life but grew up speaking French with a perfect Parisian accent, something that would be a major asset during her SOE work.

When I was born in Paris, my mother [Gertrude] wanted to call me Cecilia, not Cécile, as my first Christian name. At the town hall they wouldn't write Cecilia because they said it wasn't a French name. That's why I am called Cécile and not Cecilia. But they condescended to accept Pearl as a second name.

My father, like my mother, was from a well-to-do family. He was the son of an architect. Before he married he was secretary to a Swede who made paper for bank notes, which meant he traveled a great deal. Immediately after his studies, he led a very easy life. Not only that, but he was probably very lazy. He had no idea about taking responsibilities. In the space of nine years, he had eight children—four died very young. But he couldn't manage to give them all they needed. On top of that, he was never at home. He was a dreamer who couldn't cope; he just drifted along.

He wasn't able to waste money; he didn't have any. One of his friends who helped us financially came to see me when I was 11 or 12 years old. At the time my father was ill, and I knew he drank. Yet he couldn't pay for his drinks because he had no money. So the others paid for his drinks. I said to the friend, "If all of you, my father's friends, didn't buy him drinks, he wouldn't be in the state he's in." Well, I never saw the friend again.

People are always the same: "Do you want a drink? Have a drink. Do you fancy another? Have another." You can't imagine the misery caused by people who drink heavily. It was definitely the cause of many of our problems.

After the First World War, my father never found it in him to control his life. Having traveled all over the world, he had friends everywhere. He was very charming and spoke five languages. Every time his friends came to Paris, they said, "Let's go to see Wallace"—my father's name. He would leave home at 11 AM and come back late at night, at two in the morning. That's all we saw of him. How did we manage to live? We were in that situation and we had to cope with it.

I went to the bar where he spent most of his time to get 20 francs a day via the barman, who gave me a box of biscuits with the bank note underneath it. Otherwise, I went to one of his friends who lived on the other side of the Seine—we lived in rue Vignon, just behind Madeleine church. First, I telephoned from the hotel opposite our apartment to find out if I could go. This friend lived next to the Institut de France, quai Visconti. From rue Vignon, I crossed all the Tuileries Gardens to go to his house, so he could give me the money we needed to shop for lunch.

When Mummy came back from the British hospital after Mimi, my youngest sister, was born—the only one of us who was born in the hospital—she found there was nothing to eat at home. She breastfed the baby until her skin was completely raw under her arms and her breasts, because she couldn't cope anymore. I went to ask our druggist to let us have some baby powder [formula] to make up Mimi's bottles. Then one day he said, "I'm sorry, it's been too long since the last payment, I can't give it to you." We were also shouted at by the local baker because our bread had not been paid for in goodness knows how long. This happened in the middle of the street, when we were on our way home.

Each day at four o'clock, before the market opened, I went to rummage through a bag of rotten potatoes, to pick out the best ones. Since then, I can't stand having dirty hands or things that aren't fresh.

We were never unhappy at home with Mummy—except when she argued with my father. I couldn't bear my parents' rows [fights] and I still can't stand rows at any price. If I end up in an argument with someone, it means that I have been really pushed to my limits. Rows make me ill!

One day, when I was 12 or 13 years old, Mummy received a paper from the tax office. My father wasn't at home. We didn't know where he was. "Listen," she said to me, "you have to go to see the tax collector." There was a problem with the taxes. She couldn't take care of it herself because she didn't speak very good French and, on top of that, she was hard of hearing. So I had to go down and explain our situation to the collector and work things out by myself.

Another time, when I was coming back from a walk—we didn't go to school but we went out every day—what did we find when we got to the front door? All the furniture on the pavement. Well I played merry hell [flew into a rage]. Then I was told to shut up. I didn't understand, obviously. In fact, my father hadn't paid the rent throughout the First World War.

We lived like this until 1922. That year, my uncle, my mother's brother, came to Paris with his wife and he realized what was going on. From then on he helped my mother pay the rent.

I didn't really have any childhood, but because of the sense of responsibility that I had to have very young, the way I had to live as a child and a teenager, I became very strong and realized that I had to fight for things in life. I didn't have any choice, given the circumstances, but that was the result.

Mummy always looked on me as the support of the family. She never had to fight when she was young. She was her father's favorite; she could ask for anything and she'd get it. She never wanted for anything when she was younger, so she wasn't prepared for coping with difficulties. She accepted help from her brother, then when he died, from her brother-in-law, and she also tried to improve things by giving English lessons and so forth. But it was not enough for six people. So eventually I started to work to meet my family's needs.

When I look back I realize my mother was very strict with us, and much stricter with me than with my sisters. I'm three and a half years older than my next sister, because Mummy lost two children in between us. You know when you are young that makes a big difference. My sisters have no idea what my life was like when I was very young. Do you know how old I was when I finally got the dress I wanted? I was 27. Until then I had worn my cousin's clothes. My aunt was fond of dressmaking, and her daughter was her model. When my cousin had had enough of the clothes she wore, or when my aunt felt like making something else, she sent the clothes to Mummy. For years that's how I was dressed, but I didn't mind. I was always very happy to see new clothes arrive. There wasn't the same materialistic lifestyle there is today. Sometimes I get very sore feet: I also wore my aunt's shoes, and her feet were slightly smaller than mine. My toes are knotted. It wasn't always very comfortable.

Mummy let my younger sisters do much more than I was allowed. I don't hold it against her, it's just a fact. I realized that my youngest sisters could go out more easily than I could. They belonged to a British sports club in Paris that organized dances, and they used to pinch [steal] my clothes and accessories to go to these events, and when I needed my things, I couldn't find them. That's the sort of freedom I never had.

I learned to write French during the three years I attended school, from the age of 13 and a half to 17. The reason I started so late was because my father had intended to send me to boarding school, but he never did. I learned how to read French on my own. Do you know how? One day a lorry [truck] was driving along the rue Royale, and I suddenly realized I could read the writing on its side. I was so surprised. However, when I saw a verb in the plural, for example "ils appellent" ["they call," pronounced "eelz ah-pell"], I pronounced it "ils appelant" [eelz ah-pell-ehnt], as if it were English and all the letters had to be pronounced. I also learned shorthand.

Mummy taught me to read and write in English, some geography and history, and a little arithmetic. Don't talk to me about mathematics; I don't know anything about math. I was not very good at history but very good at geography, and hopeless at written French. I know there are substantial gaps in my schooling, but I have always managed to put up with them, so I continue to do so. These gaps forced me to work harder, to fight, in a way, for my education. Someone once said to me, "I was always told you were very hard." I replied, "It's not me; it's life."

My schooling was very different from today's. It wasn't at all the same educational system. Moreover, I was in a bilingual school; we worked in French in the morning and English in the afternoon. We had a French dictation every morning, which I had to redo as many times as I made mistakes: I made a mistake in almost every word. Gradually it sunk in that rules in French have to be remembered. We always learned by copying everything several times: there's only one "p" in "apercevoir," copied over and over again. In three years, though, I really learned how to write French, and I learned French grammar, or at least its basics. I cannot say my French is very stylish, but I hope I don't make too many mistakes in syntax. I'm just lucky because I have a photographic memory. On Thursdays [the day off from school in France at the time], Sundays, and every evening of the week I did my homework, until I was 17.

After I left school I did a type of commercial training. I passed a British Chamber of Commerce exam in French-English commercial terms and two exams in shorthand. This bilingual school [the Paris British School] was in the rue Guersant not very far from our present flat [rue Pergolèse]. It was a fee-paying school. I think the English Protestant church paid the fees, I'm not sure, but I do know that we couldn't afford to pay for it.

We lived at that time on the rue Vignon, some distance from the school. To get there we got the tram from place de la Madeleine to the avenue des Ternes. We had lunch at school—paid for by our church, I'm sure of that. When we left school at 3:30 PM, we walked all the way home.

I read a lot, but with no logical order. Sometimes I chose books, sometimes I just read the books people lent me. I didn't buy books and didn't go to libraries. I read books I found at home, books that were lent or given to me, and sometimes I received books as presents. While in school I would sometimes read in secret until two in the morning, naughty me!

One book I read just before the start of the war was the story of a woman who was an agent during the 1914–1918 war. The book was called *Louise de Bettignies: Sister in Arms* by Hélène d'Argoeuvres. Louise de Bettignies helped people escape from Belgium for France, to get away from the Germans. It made a big impression on me; I thought it was something I would like to do.

I also read *Gone with the Wind*. Another novel that made a big impression on me was *The Keys of the Kingdom* by [A. J.] Cronin. It really opened my eyes to the question of religion because it is the story of someone deeply Christian but who is repeatedly at odds with the church's administration. It left its mark on me.

When I was 17, I left school and tried to find work, but it was very difficult for foreigners. I had to have a work permit to be able to find employment, and I could only get the permit if I was employed. Finally, an Englishman who ran a well-known clothing shop in Paris that still stands on the corner of rue Saint-Honore and the rue Duphot helped me. He had often seen us walk past on our way to the Tuileries Garden, Mummy with her three girls, all dressed the same, and a baby in the pram. Everybody in the area had noticed the four little English girls. One fine day, much later, Mummy went to see him and told him about her worries for her daughter who needed a work permit.

"That's not a problem," he replied, "I'll prepare a letter and she'll get her permit."

It was very kind of him because, after all, it was a false statement. He gave me a false letter stating he employed me. This enabled me to obtain a work permit, which meant that I could look for a job.

My father had spent a lot of time in Sweden and still had friends there. The first job I had when I was 17 was with a Swedish company, a match manufacturer. I started there in September 1931. I was in the publicity department—there were advertisements on the matchboxes. But the big boss, Kruger, committed suicide because of a financial scandal. All his business affairs and the match empire collapsed, which meant that I was out of work for at least a month.

My mother asked me to collect money by selling Alexandra roses—wild roses made of fabric—to raise funds for the Hertford British Hospital in Levallois-Perret. The hospital was allowed to do this once a year and Mummy had asked for approval from a director who represented Thomas Cook and Sons, one of the oldest British travel agencies in Paris. While talking to him she happened to mention that she was looking for a job for her eldest daughter. He said he knew someone who was looking for a young person to work with the air attaché [an air force diplomat] at the British embassy in Paris.

That's how I started working at the embassy. I was taken on for a month's trial period, but at the end of it I went home and told Mummy, "They cannot keep me; they haven't received the go-ahead from London." She fainted on the spot. Luckily it worked out in the end. I worked there as a typist for seven years, earning 1,000 francs a month, giving everything to Mummy, except for what I made giving English lessons in the evenings, until the war started.

2

COURTSHIP WITH HENRI CORNIOLEY

Henri Cornioley was a French native, but his father had been born in Switzerland and his mother in Hungary. Although he and Pearl had sharply contrasting childhoods—Henri's family ran a prosperous beauty salon—they were attracted to each other when they became friends on Henri's return from his military service in Tunisia during the early 1930s.

Henri was three and a half years older than me, the brother of my childhood friend Evelyne, but I didn't see him often when we were young. That's because Henri was very ill when he was a child. The doctor thought he might have tuberculosis, so he was sent to Switzerland as a preventative measure. In fact it was diphtheria. When he returned to Paris I didn't see him then because his parents sent him to boarding school.

My first recollection of Henri was in front of the Madeleine Church. I was passing the church on the way back from the market with Mummy and my two sisters. I saw him and said to Mummy, "That's Evelyne's brother." That was it.

Years later, I was strolling down the Champs Elysées [a famous street in Paris] with Henri's brother, Charles, and Evelyne. Henri walked past. It was just before he did his military service in Tunisia [in 1930]. He didn't say hello or anything—[behaving as a typical] elder brother. But on his return from his military service, he joined our group, and that's how it all started. In fact, when it started, as far as I'm concerned anyway, we were just very close friends. But one day he suddenly made it clear that his interest in me was romantic. I said, "Hold on; we can't. In any case, I can't leave Mummy and my sisters." I was 19 when we really started courting in 1933.

We started courting—in fact we got engaged—against both our families' wishes. My mother was against it because I was her only support for the family—by this time my father had died [in 1930] and my sisters were somewhat younger than myself. Mummy definitely disapproved my leaving home.

I must add, though, my mother encountered many difficulties in France. She was never used to the type of life the family led. First, we were very isolated; she rarely had the chance to meet French people, and her one idea was to get back to England. She didn't even have enough money to pay for the journey—we had nothing, no money whatsoever. They were very difficult times.

As for Henri's father, one day while Mummy and my sisters were in Wissant by the sea—Mummy earned money then by taking small groups of children there to teach them English—he trailed me round the streets of Paris telling me his son was a good-for-nothing. I told him that, for the moment, I wasn't in a position to marry Henri, but, I said, "We're very good friends. I can't say whether one day we'll marry or not, but I won't accept not being able to see him anymore."

From then on, I wasn't allowed into Henri's house. Henri's father was against us for a number of reasons. First, he needed Henri at work. Also, Henri had confided our secret relationship with his mother; it was through her he learned about us. The third reason is that his father thought that if Henri married the eldest girl of a large family, he'd find himself responsible for the lot.

I thought all this was so unfair, and I thought Mummy would help me. But when I told her about my problems, she said, "What? Turn one of my daughters out of his house? In that case, Henri cannot come to us either."

The outcome was that we could only meet in the streets of Paris and on park benches, as in Brassen's song: "Sur les bancs publics, bancs publics . . ." ["On the public benches, the public benches . . ."]. We had our own bench on the Champs Elysées.

This lasted six years, almost until the war started. At that point, I was allowed to come to Henri's house. Henri's mother had finally won over his father. I don't know what she said, but I started visiting Henri at home before he ever came to us.

For a few years while courting we each had a diary, which we kept in turn for a week. Every day we jotted down our comments; then we swapped them at the end of the week. That went on for several years. We don't have many left. But I found one from 1937 where I hesitated between [the more intimate] *tu* [you] and [the more formal] *vous* [you]. From 1933 to 1937, I used *vous*. In 1937, I used *tu* from time to time; then I'd switch back to *vous*. Today, people start by calling you by your Christian name and by using *tu*.

Henri and I played tennis, in 1933 or '34, in Aubervilliers. We also went to the cinema, in winter, on Sunday mornings. It was a bit warmer than sitting on benches. We had just enough money to pay for the news films. There was one cinema open, the Berlitz Palace; we went there. We saw the news film and a cartoon, or something similar. There was no television at the time, so small cinemas showed the weekly news and one or two cartoons. The big cinemas showed the news and a feature film. It was warm in there, and the films went on for a long time. You could stay as long as you liked, you just paid to get in once. We knew the Berlitz Palace inside out. Usually we walked along the *grands boulevards* [main streets] to get there.

During Henri's leave from the military in February 1940, my mother invited Henri to our house. After that, Henri and I didn't see each other for three and a half years, because of the war, until the end of 1943.

3

ESCAPE FROM FRANCE

Pearl and Henri were forced to separate when Henri was called up for military service in 1939, the year the Nazis invaded Poland and both Great Britain and France declared war on Germany. During the eight months of uneventful tension that followed—called the Drôle de Guerre (Phony War or Silly War)—Henri and Pearl saw each other only once, when Henri was on leave in February 1940. Then, during the Battle of France, which occurred during May and June of 1940, Henri was taken prisoner by the Germans (for more about Henri's wartime experiences, see "Henri's Story" in the appendix, page 133), and Pearl and her family made two harrowing attempts to escape the country.

The family's first trip—straight west from Paris to Normandy—occurred when the Germans first crossed the French border during the Battle of France, causing a panic among the civilians. The French government had not expected the Germans to break through their military defenses as quickly as they did and so had not created an evacuation plan for most of their population. So between six and eight million French people took matters into their own hands and fled in a panic, starting in the northeast and north central parts of the country and working their way south, southwest, and west in what immediately became known as the Exodus. The fears of the French were based mainly on horrible memories of German brutality that had occurred during the First World War, when northeastern France had been occupied by the Germans.

After the armistice was signed with Germany and France was divided into two zones—the north and western occupied zone and the southern free, or unoccupied, zone—most French people, including Pearl and her family, returned to their homes from their initial flight, somewhat relieved that their fears of random German brutality toward the defeated French now seemed exaggerated.

However, Pearl and her family had more to fear than most of their neighbors. They were British citizens, and although defeated France was no longer considered an enemy by the Germans, Great Britain still was. When Pearl heard at the beginning of December that the Germans were planning to arrest British citizens close to her area, she and her family attempted to flee Paris again. All the crucial decisions and bureaucratic technicalities that were part of trying to quickly escape Nazi-overrun France when many others were trying to do the same thing were always Pearl's responsibility.

Their journeys were not easy. Their initial flight to Normandy had exhausted their savings. When they finally arrived there, they were told to wait for instructions from British embassy officials regarding their passage to England. But while they waited, the Germans arrived. When the instructions finally came, they were told that passage would not be provided for them.

The second trip, beginning in the winter of 1940, was long and difficult, and they occasionally traveled on foot. The map on page 29 shows the probable route they took with all its twists, turns, reverses, detours, and challenges.

Though Pearl's family received some money from the American and British embassies—and Pearl worked temporarily for the British embassy in one city along the way—it's difficult to imagine exactly how they were able to cope during the 13 months spanned by the following account.

Because I was a typist at the British embassy in Paris prior to 1940, I had a diplomatic identity card. In May 1940, when the Germans broke through the defense line and entered France, the ambassador asked us to evacuate Paris and wait for instructions. He and his close colleagues moved to Tours.

I went to Commes, near Port-en-Bessin [on the Normandy coast] with my mother and sisters. The Germans arrived soon afterward. We were completely panicked. I had an argument with my mother, because I didn't want to leave before my instructions arrived. But the Germans got there first. The ambassador had instructed all his staff to leave Paris. The ambassador and his attachés managed to sail from Saint-Jean-de-Luz. I was a local employee, so I had nowhere to go in England. We were blocked, there was no petrol, no trains running, and we had no money. That was such an intense period in our lives that I still have difficulty talking about it. Even after all these years, it gets stuck in my throat.

I waited in Commes for the train services to start again, and in July, I left Bayeux for Paris. I went to the American embassy in Paris to explain our situation and asked them for money. Through the embassy at Vichy, they contacted the Air Ministry in London, who asked them [the American embassy] to help me and my family as much as possible.

During all that time I was gone, my mother and sisters had to sign in every day at a German post in Port-en-Bessin. Then the Germans decided to arrest and lock up all foreigners within 18 miles of the coast. My mother and my sisters were nearly locked up in Falaise. They managed to slip through the net with the help of a French colonel who spoke German. He was an interpreter at the Kommandatur [military headquarters set up by the Germans] in Bayeux. Even though he knew who we were—British subjects trying to escape from the Germans—he helped without hesitation. Mummy and my sisters joined me in Paris in August. The American embassy had advanced an allowance, which enabled us to exist.

In Paris, I found myself surrounded by Germans; they were all over the place. They played music, and people would go and listen to them! All along rue de Rivoli, as far as you could see from place de la Concorde, there were enormous swastika banners five or six floors high. I just thought, This is impossible.

One morning, at the beginning of December, some of my sisters' friends arrived in a panic: the Germans were rounding up all the English in the 16th arrondissement [district]. We lived in the 9th arrondissement. Mummy said, "I don't want to be taken by the Germans, we're leaving." So my mother, two sisters, and I took refuge with two French families, while I tried to find a way of crossing the demarcation line into unoccupied France.

We managed to get some rather vague information. I told the police station where we had to sign on as British citizens,

"We're leaving Paris." The policeman said he would put the register aside for a couple of days to give us time to get away. We left on December 9, 1940. We took the train to Vichy, where there was an American embassy in the unoccupied zone [there was another in occupied Paris]. The Americans were not yet at war. We had to cross the demarcation line clandestinely, because we weren't allowed a pass. I was looking for any possible solution when I heard a traveler in the train compartment saying that he was taking horses across the line. I thought, There's our answer. When he stood up, I followed him down the corridor and asked him if he would accept to take four Englishwomen across. He agreed right away. We changed our route to follow him to Montceau-les-Mines, then we took a country lane. We had to hide in a ditch when a German patrol went past. Our fellow traveler paid for everything: the extra train fare and even our "coffee"—grilled barley drink—in the station "café."

The embassy in Vichy sent us to Marseille, where we stayed for three months before obtaining the papers that enabled us to go back to England via Spain and Portugal. All the English soldiers who had escaped from occupied France were grouped at Fort Saint-Jean in Marseille. An English diplomat from the American consulate had asked me if I could help organize a boat journey to take refugees to England, with Italy and Germany's authorization. It took us two months to prepare everything; then in the end the Germans said no, so it didn't come off. That diplomat spent a lot of his time helping escaping English, and I realized that something was going on.

After our departure from Marseille we went through Cerbère-Portbou [two towns, the first in France, the second in Spain, separated by a steep hill but joined by a half-mile railway tunnel]. There we were received by a representative of the British embassy who gave us some Spanish money so that we could go on to Barcelona. It was an advance: he asked us for reimbursement on our arrival in England.

To get into Spain one had to have either US dollars, which cost an arm and a leg, or pesetas, Spanish currency. When we went through customs in Spain they asked us whether we had anything to declare. Reply: nothing. We had no more money. One of the female staff began to undress Mummy. She put a hand in her corset: I wish you could have seen Mummy's face at that moment. I said to her, "What are you looking for"?

"Money."

"I told you, we haven't got any."

"I have never seen English people traveling without any money."

"Have you never heard of refugees?" I replied.

The train between Portbou and Barcelona was stuffed full. You saw everything in the trains at that time, including cages of hens. We were not in the same compartment: Mummy was with one of my sisters and I was in another compartment with the other sister. I simply could not get near the restaurant car. We had to wait until the next stop to get something to eat. We ran to join Mummy; there we were very close to the restaurant car. But the waiter would not let us in because our ticket was for the preceding service. We had to negotiate. Some young Spanish army officers who spoke French took us under their wing and eventually we were able to eat.

We spent the following night in Madrid. We had the address of a Spanish family we were supposed to go and see to give them news of a niece, married to a Frenchman, whom we knew well in Paris. Unfortunately, on the way back, we crossed a square without using the zebra crossing [crosswalk]. There weren't many cars, but we were bawled out by a Spanish policeman. It was awful. I said, *"No comprende; Inglés . . ."* Eventually, he didn't fine us. We found somewhere where there were no cars, and all three of us crossed together.

We crossed Spain via Barcelona and Madrid, stayed for another three months in Portugal. As I had worked in Paris for the air attaché, I managed to find the same kind of work in the British embassy in Lisbon. It gave us a bit of money, luckily, because we didn't have much.

Normally I would have gone to the British embassy in Madrid. Don't ask me why I didn't. It must have been fate. If I had, I would have gone no further because they were on the lookout for embassy staff, to employ them. But then destiny is curious, isn't it?

When we reached Lisbon I went to see the air attaché to ask him to send a message to London, announcing our arrival. There also, they were looking for embassy staff to employ.

According to the exchanges between England and Portugal, I ought to have gone to Madrid. I did not want to do that at all. I wanted to stay with Mummy and my two sisters. We spent three months in Lisbon. They were so insistent that I stay at the embassy that I wasn't at all sure that I would be able to return to England; that's why I did not register for the boat. I did it at the last minute and so I couldn't travel in the same cabin as my mother and sisters.

In the meantime, the staff from the British embassy in Yugoslavia had arrived in Madrid as refugees. They were grabbed [pressured to work for the embassy], and it was they who had to stay there while I took the boat with Mummy. That happened at the end of June 1941.

I set foot in a nightclub for the first time in my life in Portugal. We even stayed up all night once because some of my sisters' friends wanted to see the sunrise on mount Sintra. Portugal wasn't at war, so there were lights everywhere. It was wonderful. Also, there were no shortages. There was a mix of anyone you can imagine: Allies, Germans. . . . We were there from March to May.

We took a banana boat from the port in Lisbon and arrived in Gibraltar four or five days later. The passengers had to bring their own food; we ate sardines for the entire trip. We slept where we could: on the bridge, in the hold, elsewhere. In Gibraltar we were put on board the *Scythia*, which was moored at a detached mole; that is to say, on a faraway quay. It was a liner that had come from South Africa with a great many officers on board, mainly airmen. There were not enough places in England to train all the airmen—and it was dangerous there as well—so many of them went to South Africa for their training.

The banana boat on which we had arrived returned to Lisbon; we had to wait until it came back with another cargo of refugees. We remained at anchor in Gibraltar for at least two weeks. When the *Scythia* left, another ship joined it. We made the crossing to Scotland in a convoy of only 2 ships, instead of the usual 22. There were at least three warships surrounding us. I suppose we were carrying a particularly important cargo.

When we got near the Scottish coast we were joined by a cruiser. Having left Paris on December 9, 1940, we arrived in London on July 14, 1941. From the beginning to the end of that seven-month journey, we always found help. Long before we began talking about the word "resistance," there were French people who were fundamentally and morally opposed to the occupation. It was those people who helped my mother, my sisters, and me to escape to England.

When I arrived in London, I started by settling my mother in a rented flat, and my sisters joined the WAAF [Women's Auxiliary Air Force]. I contacted the administration services of the air attachés. For two years I was personal assistant to the director of Allied Air Forces and Foreign Liaison.

It was nearly impossible for Henri and I to communicate while I was in England, but we managed to do so. I was at the Air Ministry, in the department which was responsible for all the foreign air forces based in England. The sections included France, Poland, Czechoslovakia, and so on, and there was a security section. In December 1940, just before I left Paris, I managed to get Henri's address. At that time he was a prisoner in Germany. When I left Lisbon to go to England, with my mother and sisters, I gave Henri's address to a colleague who was half-English, half-Portuguese. She worked in the embassy press office. As her name was Portuguese, it helped vis-à-vis German censorship. I also left her some money and asked her to be kind enough to send a Red Cross parcel to Henri from time to time. The Portuguese Red Cross was able to send parcels to prisoners of war for which there was a charge. Henri didn't suspect that I'd sent them. I think it was via his grandmother in Lausanne [Switzerland] that Henri learned I was in England. We could write to Switzerland, they weren't at war.

When I arrived in England, I learned that Henri had escaped from Germany to unoccupied France; correspondence was possible between Portugal and unoccupied France. I came to an arrangement with the department's security section. They asked the English censorship office to read my unsealed letters but not to mark them CENSORED. Normally each letter was opened, read, then closed with a sticker saying CENSORED. So I gave them my letters, they sealed them, and the letters were put in the diplomatic bag for Lisbon. My friend in Portugal, to whom the outside envelope was addressed, opened it, and inside was a letter for Henri in the unoccupied zone. She would put Portuguese stamps on, and when the letter went through the German censorship, it looked as if it had come from Portugal.

Thus we kept in touch up to 1942, until the North African landing. That's when London put a stop to it.

We used this method for lots of letters, in both directions. We even have an envelope that was censored twice, which is unique in history. The Germans had their own censorship and they also cut bits out. When they found something they didn't like, they crossed it out and you couldn't read it. If that's not a dictatorship I don't know what is. Dictatorship is something I cannot abide, whatever kind. This letter was censored by the Germans when it was sent and by the English on arrival, which is why it's unique, because there was no correspondence between France and England.

4

TRAINING AND PREPARATION IN THE RANKS OF THE SOE

At first, some within the ranks of the SOE, including the F Section, balked at the idea of including women. But because men in Nazi-occupied countries were expected to be employed in German munitions factories, male SOE agents posing as regular citizens would immediately come under suspicion. Women were ideal candidates for the SOE roles of couriers and radio operators because they could move about more freely than their male counterparts without arousing as much suspicion.

Although many of the SOE women nominally joined the First Aid Nursing Yeomanry (FANY) as a cover for their actual role in the SOE, Pearl, along with 14 others of the 39 female F Section agents, remained technically part of the Women's Auxiliary Air Force (WAAF). Pearl had already been working for the WAAF in a clerical position.

During her SOE training, Pearl was given an honorary commission in the WAAF and given the rank of a second lieutenant. It was hoped (in vain, it turned out) that, if captured, the enemy would treat these "officers" as POWs according to the Geneva convention.

SOE superiors were very selective in choosing their agents, knowing not only that if they sent the wrong type of person into an occupied country they would be sending that agent to certain death but also that the wrong candidate would endanger the lives of everyone he or she worked with. The candidates underwent weeks of training together in country houses in the north of England and Scotland, during which time they were closely scrutinized for personal traits that would either help or hinder their work and that of their fellow agents.

Pearl made a very positive impression on most of her SOE instructors. Although one of them suggested that she would succeed only under the guidance of a strong leader, the others were more complimentary. One of them said that Pearl, "though a woman, has definitely got leaders' qualities" and that she was "cool and resourceful and extremely determined." Her field craft instructor said that Pearl had "plenty of intelligence and makes use of it," while her weapons trainer said that Pearl was "probably the best shot (male or female) we have yet had." He also noted that Pearl had a "sound knowledge of weapons and stripping," something that would serve her well during her second wave of Resistance work. Another instructor noted that Pearl was "very capable, completely brave and would far prefer to participate in an active, rather than passive, role."

knew that I could help in the war effort, even if I didn't know exactly how things were going to work out. But I thought that I could be much more useful in France, pushing the Germans out, than in England doing paperwork. I applied to the Inter-Services Research Bureau via the head of the air attachés, who was a friend and my former boss at the British embassy in Paris. It wasn't easy. The regular army, led by professional officers, didn't like the Inter-Services Research Bureau at all—to them that bureau was just a bunch of amateurs. My former boss said to me one day, "You are not going to work with those people!" And he stopped me from entering the bureau. I thought, What a nerve! I had already decided that it was what I wanted to do.

I explained my problem to a friend from the embassy in Paris who I had met again in London. She said, "Don't worry." I knew that she worked for the Foreign Office, but I didn't know that she was the minister's secretary! I had the feeling that she had something to do with the service in which I was interested, but I didn't know its real name. In fact, the Inter-Services Research Bureau was the Special Operations Executive, the SOE, whose name we only learned many years after the war. A meeting was arranged for me with Colonel [Maurice] Buckmaster, who was head of the French section of the SOE. That's how the ball started rolling.

The French section of the SOE recruited in England by first identifying people who spoke French. To start with they didn't tell them why they were being interviewed—I found that out during my training. Whereas I knew perfectly well what I wanted to do. During our attempts to escape France I was slightly exposed to some resistance movements in Marseille.

Maurice Southgate was an old school friend, British-born but French educated, like me, and had attended the same Paris British School as I had. He had become an interior designer who had trained at the École Boulle. When, in 1939, Maurice

Southgate came to the British embassy in Paris to join the RAF, we bumped into each other at the entrance. We had not seen each other for a very long time.

We agreed to meet later, but he was taken on as a sergeant interpreter with the RAF in Rheims. We completely lost contact until we met again in London in 1941, when I started at the Air Ministry. He had already been there almost a year. One day I said to him, "You know, I intend to go back to France to help the resistance. Would you like to do that?"

"I don't know anything about it."

"I can help you if you like."

"Give me 24 hours to think about it, I'll tell you tomorrow."

His wife was in France, he was in England, and I knew he was bored. The next day he agreed. He started his training before me. When the time came for him to leave for France, I asked him to contact Henri, to tell him that I would join him. I would have liked Henri to come to England so that we could train together and both go to France as a team. I had sent him a coded message, advising him to "go on a cure of oranges"—in other words, to go to Spain in order to come to England—but he didn't understand. But as soon as I was sure that Henri had received Maurice's message, I volunteered.

We started with three weeks paramilitary training handling arms, explosives, learning how to fall on landing, and so on. There were 17 of us, including 3 women.

Then I spent seven weeks shut up in one of the special SOE schools. Training focused on the life of a secret agent and the necessary skills for surviving in France. We started the day with physical training at 7 AM and worked until late in the evening. When they had finished with me I was exhausted!

As an exercise, I was sent to Birmingham [a city about 120 miles from London] with a false identity card to try to recruit other "resistant fighters." I had trouble knowing where I was because there, like everywhere in England, all the sign posts had been taken down to prevent any German parachutists finding their way. From the second night on, I had to find a room on my own. I asked a milkman on his daily round if he knew of a good place; he knew his way 'round all the houses and knew everyone.

We were also sent to Manchester, in the north of England, to learn how to parachute. One of the boys said to me, "You'll see, it's an extraordinary experience. You feel the whole world belongs to you." But it's not true! I was quickly back on the ground and the second time I fell more heavily than the first, as if I had fallen 10 feet.

When we started our training, everyone learned Morse code. I was desperate because I couldn't do it. I thought, If I can't do it, they won't send me! When I was a Girl Guide [English Girl Scouts], we had learned semaphore [a visual code method of communication] with flags and I saw the letters instead of hearing them.

Finally one day, I was so worried I went to see the commandant of the school. I said, "It's impossible, it's hellish this Morse, I can't do it, I just can't do it."

"Well," he replied, "you don't need to worry about it. Why get in a state about it? If you can't, you can't."

What a relief! I was convinced that I had to learn it in case the radio operator I worked with was caught or couldn't do his work. I thought I absolutely had to be able to replace him, but it wasn't like that at all. The school simply wanted to know if we were capable of doing the Morse code, and if so, we carried on in that line.

We were also taught unarmed combat. When they said, "If you're attacked you've got to do such and such a thing," I thought, Right, if I'm attacked, I'll try. In other words, I took in everything they said without questioning it; not once did I think it was daft or pointless.

But I never would have been able to use a weapon against someone in cold blood. I think that's a feminine issue. I think women are made to give life, not to take it. But I might have defended myself with an arm [weapon] if I had been obliged to. Our training was very good on the whole, and I took it all in because I was convinced it would help me in the job I had to do, but I never was in a critical situation where I needed to fight, one on one. But several times since the war, I've wondered what would happen if some poor chap tried to attack me in the street. I'm sure I would knock him out—I wouldn't be able to stop myself!

During our training we were told that if we were arrested and interrogated to try to resist for 48 hours to give the others a chance to escape. You don't know how you might react under torture. If someone starts pulling off your toenails or you are plunged in and out of a bath, you can't say, "I won't talk"; it's impossible to predict your reaction. Yet some people did resist. Some died because of it.

Secrecy was the key word during our training. Even my family didn't know where I was or what I was doing. We weren't allowed to tell anyone. I didn't know what my best friends were doing. To find something out during the war you had to belong to that particular department, but even then you were not completely in the know. Even the army didn't realize that we were civilians in uniform. During training I was given a uniform and the rank of second lieutenant. Right, I thought, I am a second lieutenant. In fact, it was only an honorary commission. It was a sort of military cover that, it was hoped, would give some protection if we were captured, but in fact I was still a civilian.

To become an officer in England during the war, you had to spend at least six months in the ranks. Time was too short for the agents to actually become part of the military.

One thing that made me wretched was wondering what would happen to Mummy if I didn't come back. I asked to see Vera Atkins, the intelligence officer under Colonel Buckmaster, to find out what would happen in that event. She said I had to ask the colonel. So I did, but to no avail. He said, "What would your mother do if a bomb fell on you in London?" His reply didn't satisfy me, so I went to the RAF to see my former boss from the British embassy, Douglas Colyer. He promised he would do whatever was necessary.

5

PARACHUTING INTO OCCUPIED FRANCE

Pearl specifically requested to join the Stationer network or circuit, which was headed by her old school friend Maurice Southgate (whose code name was "Hector Stationer"). The Stationer network's mission, like most other SOE-run networks in France, was stated as "harassment." Used in a military sense, this means to exhaust or impede an enemy. The operatives were to hinder the German war effort in any way possible, but specifically they worked to destroy communication lines, transportation methods, and munitions production, especially in preparation for D-Day. To this end, they sought to recruit, organize, supply, and train groups of Maquis within their network in southern France (the demarcation line between occupied France and unoccupied France ran across Stationer's northern border).

The political and military affiliation of the Maquis groups within the Stationer circuit was varied but

Southgate, one of SOE's most effective organizers, found a way to make it work. Many Maquis recruited by the Stationer network were from the Communist Francs-Tireurs et Partisans (FTP), fighters who normally only took orders from Communists. But Auguste Chantraine—the mayor of Tendu and a Communist who had agreed to help the SOE—was in charge of Stationer's northern section, and he was able to recruit Communist Maquis into Stationer.

Charles Rechenmann, a former member of the French military who could recruit other former military men, was put in charge of Stationer's southern section.

Part of the SOE training was practicing parachuting since most SOE agents—like Pearl—parachuted into remote rural areas of occupied France near the time of a full moon. After the agents had left England for work in the field it was very disappointing to have to turn back due to bad weather or problems with the landing party that was to meet them on the ground. Some agents gave up completely after multiple failed attempts to jump, feeling that they were somehow unlucky. Pearl—who had to turn back twice before landing in France—didn't.

Henri joined the Stationer circuit before Pearl arrived. On the night of Pearl's first attempt to parachute in, Maurice Southgate arrived in the landing area only to discover that the French police had been unusually active there, searching for FTP Maquis. He needed to contact the SOE in London immediately so that Pearl's flight could be canceled in time.

Maurice Southgate sent Henri on a frantic 20-kilometer bicycle ride to radio operator Amédée Maingard so that he could contact London. But the two men hadn't met before, and by the time Amédée had finished questioning Henri to make sure he could be trusted (in other words, that he wasn't either a Milice or a Gestapo agent) it was too late to tell London to cancel the flight. The only way to prevent Pearl's landing now would be to remove the drop zone lights and hope the pilot would understand.

During my first attempt at landing, the night of September 15–16, we made a round trip. The landing strip was in the north of Indre. They hadn't put the lamps on the ground to mark the strip, which meant that I couldn't jump. Maurice Southgate had made the decision because the area had suddenly become a dangerous place for dropping in an agent; the gendarmerie [French police] were looking for three leaders of the Francs-Tireurs et Partisans in the woods at Taille de Ruine. I returned to Tempsford, my starting point.

The second attempt was in the night of September 21–22. I had quite a fright before takeoff, when the plane was maneuvering on the runway. I didn't understand what was going on. The engines were getting louder and louder, which was quite normal, but then suddenly, the noise stopped. I looked at the dispatcher and asked him, "What's happening?" No one was laughing. He said, "This isn't a real runway." The landing strip was in a field belonging to a farm and probably wasn't very wide. One of the wheels had run off the strip, so we had to start all over again.

The weather was so bad that night that we couldn't even go back to our base, Tempsford. We landed in an aerodrome called Ford, on the south coast of England. I was with two Frenchmen.

There were also homing pigeons in the plane in a little box, with a parachute. They were for the intelligence service. The pigeons should have been dropped to an agreed spot so that messages could be attached to them and taken back to England. Well, that evening, they didn't even drop the pigeons. The weather was so bad that they had no idea where we were.

When I entered the military base, everyone inside looked at me as if I were a strange animal. They were young, and it was one or two o'clock in the morning. Nobody was expecting to see a lady out of uniform at that time of night. This incongruity was explained by saying that I was a reporter.

Then someone said, "Right, you can go to the dining room." I headed there, trying to be as inconspicuous as possible, when an officer in British uniform started talking to me in French. He was very charming, Philippe Livry-Level, a famous French airman [and veteran of the 1914–1918 war] who so desperately wanted to be a pilot during this war that he had lied about his age [he was eight years too old] and managed to join the Royal Air Force. The RAF eventually found out, but they kept him as a navigator. Livry-Level must have been in the teams flying between France and England. When I was talking to him I had the impression that he knew perfectly well why I was there.

While we were waiting to get back to our base I was given an airman's bedroom. It wasn't very pleasant and I didn't sleep much. It was freezing cold and it also smelled awful! You know how some people have a strange smell. Anyway, I thought to myself, I have a room, I can't complain.

We left the next morning. The funny thing was, I had come with a team of petty officers who were really pleased to escort a "bird" around! I thought that I was going to return with them, but a squadron leader arrived and said, "I'll take her." I had to go back with him. After all, what else could I do? I didn't have any say in the matter.

During the flight from Ford to Tempsford, the squadron leader told me to go to the front of the plane. The nose of the bomber, as well as the rear, had a clear plastic bay window for the machine-gunners. He told me to lie in there on my tummy. Through the plastic I could see everything that went by. When we were flying over a fairly tall chimney, he said, "You'll see what happens when we fly over it." There was a *whoosh* and we dropped because of the mass of rising warm air. It was quite bizarre.

The crossing was not as fast as it is today, despite the four engines! There were 400 to 500 miles, which meant almost two hours of flying.

My third attempt at a parachute landing was successful. Just in time! It was the night of September 22–23, 1943, and the last night of the moon. If I had not been able to jump then, I would have had to wait another month. Our pilots needed the moonlight to see the rivers, which acted as landmarks. When they headed south of the Loire, they flew near Blois, where there are three rivers, the Loir, Loire, and Cher.

They flew that way frequently, so they knew the route very well, but they were just as frequently attacked by flak—anti-aircraft guns—which tossed the plane. We were not hit that night because we were too high, but the plane was shaken by the explosions. At first I wondered what was happening, but the dispatcher reassured me, "Don't worry," he said, "it's the flak; we're used to it."

I was in a massive Halifax bomber, equipped to go as far as Poland. Usually, there were long seats running down the middle of the fuselage, opposite each other, where one could lie down.

But this time the space was taken up by fuel tanks. It's a long way to Poland and back!

The crew had kindly found me a sleeping bag and I lay down in it, on the floor, waiting for the moment to jump. Although the noise was terrible because of the four engines, I managed to sleep. I hadn't slept the night before, due to the previous unsuccessful landing.

Around midnight, I began sitting for quite a long time on the edge of the opening I would have to jump through. It wasn't very warm. The plane circled for a long time while I was waiting there, and I didn't know why. But in a plane the size of a Halifax bomber, it isn't easy to pinpoint four little electric torches [flashlights] on the ground. I thought that the torches were always held by hand, but this time, the reception committee had done something different. They had three small torches on the ground, with the fourth one a bit further along, staggered a little to indicate the direction of the wind. At the same time, the fourth torch gave the letter of the landing strip in Morse code. That was essential—if they had not given the right letter, I would have had to go back.

I just waited for the red light to come on. It wasn't like our training sessions, when the dispatcher would shout "Action station!" with me on the edge of the hole, in the middle of the fuselage, ready to jump, and then "Go!" He would shout very loudly so there was no hesitation, we just did it. This was different. There were two lights: the green one meant "get ready" and the red one "go."

When the red light came on, well, off I went. The hole I jumped through was like a downward chimney. You had to jump with your legs together, as if you were jumping vertically into water, at the same time keeping your arms by your side, clutching your trousers. The parachute was attached to the plane, it's known as a static line. The folds of the parachute were held together with small strings, you could really feel them snapping during the descent. When the last string snapped off, the parachute opened, it jerked a little.

During the fall, in our training, we had to reach up the harness as far as possible and pull the parachute down toward ourselves, that way we landed leaning slightly over to one side. We landed on the right or the left, which prevented us tumbling head-over-heels and getting tangled in the cords. That's how we had been taught to fall.

I had done one night fall during training, and the landing is not as hard as during the day, apparently due to heat rising from the ground. We didn't know what to expect underneath us in the dark, and although I suppose there were possible dangers with night landing, I never thought about them. I was convinced I just had to get on with it.

The plane crew took care of my luggage, which was dropped through the same hole. Because of the wind, I landed in some bushes. I thought, That's it, I've been blown off course by the wind, I'm not where I should be. And the parachute would not collapse because of the wind. During our training, we had been told that if this happened, we had to move round the parachute to collapse it. But I couldn't do it, I ended up twisting my ankles—it was awful—so I took the device holding the harness, I turned the clasp, and I gave it a thump. The parachute then came off and got tangled in the bushes. Then I thought, Right, now I must sort myself out.

I was wearing overalls, a padded helmet, and there were bandages around my ankles. I took the whole lot off and folded them into a bundle so as not to lose them. After the deafening din in the plane, the contrast was striking. There wasn't a sound to be heard and I couldn't see a thing because of the clouds.

I tried to get my bearings in the dark. Moving forward, I saw something through the bushes. It was smooth and flat and at ground level. I thought it must be the landing strip, but no, it was water. I was horrified to see water so near. In fact, I had landed between two lakes. I realized much later, when we returned, that there were two lakes and several electricity pylons and cables. Yet, surprisingly, the landing strip was often used in full safety and with no mishap.

Actually, they hadn't mentioned lakes to us during training. They had talked about the sea. Luckily, I could swim, so I probably would have managed in any case. But the satchel I was wearing was fairly heavy, and there was a sort of pocket in the overalls I was wearing, with all the most important things inside. In the end, that's all I managed to keep with me.

I was always frightened the moment I jumped; I wasn't frightened afterward. When I landed, good heavens, I was so thirsty! Not a drop of saliva in my mouth.

Then all of a sudden I remembered that I had a flask. So I thought, Why not try the flask? It was rum, how awful. I really didn't appreciate that at all.

The greeting party consisted of two men: Maurice Southgate and Auguste Chantraine, mayor of Tendu and councilor for the district. They whistled to find me [a code of two descending notes]. It was a dark night and they hadn't really seen where I had landed. I whistled back and that's how they found me.

Although I already knew Maurice, we didn't talk about anything at all. Maurice just asked me, "Did you see where your bags fell?"

I said, "Listen, it was enough working out how I was going to land myself. I've no idea, I didn't see them."

My bags had fallen in the water. I only managed to retrieve them three weeks later.

We went to Chantraine's farm. Maurice accompanied me to a barn and, pointing to a pile of hay, said, "Right, you can rest up there." I climbed the ladder and settled down on top, completely dressed. I didn't sleep much. When I came down, Maurice said, laughing, "You know, you were asleep on a pile of supplies in there." They were war supplies of course. There were at least 20 tons stacked under me, but I didn't know that.

I'm not sure what he did while I was sleeping, but he must have examined my papers to check that I had the right ration books, identity card, and so on. Then he probably took the papers I had brought for him. And there must have been some money for him, as there was for me.

In the morning, he woke me up and said, "We're leaving." We took a little train, I don't know where. I don't think I even looked at the name of the station, or maybe he arranged for me not to see it. We got out of the train at Châteauroux.

Still leading the way, he took me to the Hôtel du Faisan: it was the best place. Maurice always chose the best. Henri was waiting for me, jittering like mad, as if he were the one to have parachuted. I wasn't trembling, but he was. It was the shock, the emotion of meeting again after not seeing each other for three years. We had breakfast there, then Maurice left; I don't know where. When he returned, he said, "I have a room in Limoges. You can spend the night there." And he asked Henri to take me. Henri accompanied me to the room in Limoges then immediately left for Paris.

I didn't have anything, no nightgown, nothing, because all my bags were lost. It didn't matter, I slept in my petticoat. I was very tired. Good heavens! I slept until at least eleven o'clock the next morning. When I woke up I thought, That's strange, it seems there are fleas. I got up; no doubt about it, there are fleas! But I couldn't see them in the bed, where were they? I had slept on an army of fleas that were under the bolster! It was awful, they jumped everywhere. I hadn't even felt the bites and they had completely attacked both shoulders. That's how I was welcomed to Limoges. That day, Maurice came to take me to a safe house in Riom, in Auvergne.

I was dressed in French clothing given to me by the organization's official tailor. They issued everything: my underwear as well as two suits, one grey and one brown, so the accessories could blend easily with both suits. There were no trousers at the time. There weren't any silk stockings either, you couldn't get them. We were issued cotton stockings.

The SOE were meticulous about their agents' clothes. They checked the labels and took them out or replaced them to make sure the Germans couldn't identify their origin. But there was one thing that they couldn't provide: French shoes. English shoes were quite different. Luckily, I eventually found, with the help of my sister-in-law, a less obvious pair, little material boots with cork soles. They were better, also because I had such cold feet in winter during my train journeys.

6

COURIER MISSIONS, CODE NAMES, AND COVERS

After Pearl finally arrived, the Stationer circuit had approximately 20 members who were headed by an SOE-trained group of four: Maurice Southgate, leader/organizer; Amédée Maingard, radio operator and assistant organizer; Jacqueline Nearne, a courier who parachuted in with Maurice in January 1943; and Pearl.

The area covered by Stationer was large partly because it worked closely and cooperated—liaised—with several nearby Resistance networks. Sometimes Pearl's courier work overlapped with liaison work with these networks on behalf of Stationer. The Stationer network had liaised most closely with the Headmaster network, and a few months before Pearl's arrival, Headmaster's leaders had been arrested. Stationer filled in the gap, making the work of the already large network even larger and the trips for its couriers longer. By the time Pearl landed in France, Stationer was assisting Headmaster's Maquis groups under the leadership of Henri Ingrand in Auvergne and Jacques Dufour (code named "Anastasie") in the Dordogne region, near Limoges.

Because they worked out in the open, couriers were greatly at risk for capture, interrogation, and death if they were found with Resistance materials. This is why many couriers, Pearl included, tried to memorize their information when they could. But sometimes it was not possible to memorize everything: although addresses, messages, and even timetables for parachute drops and agent pickups could be memorized, sometimes couriers had to transport more complex items such as grid references, maps, or items that couldn't fit into a pocket.

Although all SOE agents entering occupied countries acquired new identities—including a new name, a new personal history, and a pretense of new employment—that they had to memorize until the details were second nature, couriers perhaps had an especial need of them since they were constantly out in public.

I worked as a courier under Maurice Southgate for seven months. He was incredibly security minded. He was so strict about security that when he sent me somewhere, he never explained the whys and wherefores. He never used one word more than was necessary. He would tell me where to go, who to see, and what to say, and I never tried to find out more. If I had been arrested and interrogated, I had absolutely no background

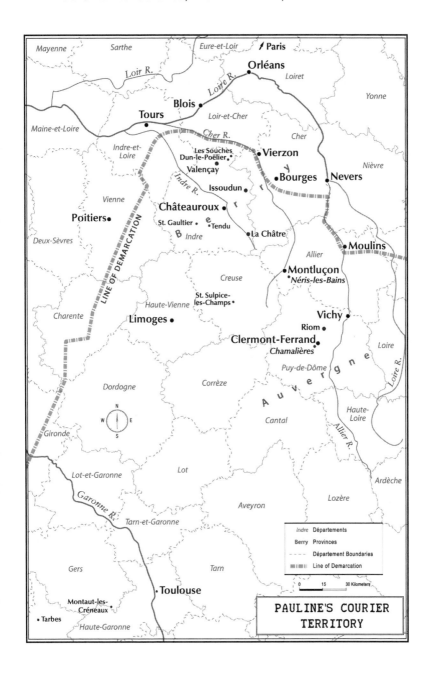

Mayenne
Sarthe
Eure-et-Loir
Paris
Orléans
Loiret
Loir R.
Loire R.
Yonne
Blois
Tours
Loir-et-Cher
Cher R.
Cher
Maine-et-Loire
Indre-et-Loire
Les Souches
Dun-le-Poëlier
Vierzon
Valençay
Nièvre
Issoudun
Bourges Nevers
Vienne
Châteauroux
Poitiers
St. Gaultier
Tendu
Deux-Sèvres
Indre
La Châtre
Allier
Moulins
Creuse
Montluçon
Néris-les-Bains
St. Sulpice-les-Champs
Haute-Vienne
Charente
Limoges
Vichy
Riom
Clermont-Ferrand
Chamalières
Loire
Puy-de-Dôme
Dordogne
Corrèze
Auvergne
Gironde
Haute-Loire
Lot-et-Garonne
Lot
Ardèche
Garonne R.
Aveyron
Lozère
Tarn-et-Garonne
Cantal
Gers
Tarn
Toulouse
Montaut-les-Créneaux
Tarbes
Haute-Garonne

LINE OF DEMARCATION

N W E S

Indre	Départements
Berry	Provinces
- - -	Département Boundaries
▪▪▪▪	Line of Demarcation

0   15   30 Kilometers

PAULINE'S COURIER
TERRITORY

information about my work and, except occasionally, I didn't need any.

For instance, when I asked him where I had landed he replied, "Luant," but it wasn't Luant at all, it was Tendu. I discovered that much later. He said this most likely to protect Monsieur Chantraine, who owned the land where I parachuted.

One day Maurice said to me, "Go to Poitiers, we haven't had any news from . . . " and he gave the name of someone I didn't know. "Go to the bursar's office at this address. You don't need to speak to anyone, go past the desk and straight to the first floor."

I left Montluçon for Poitiers. I must have arrived in the morning because I was there all day. Well, I got to the address, went in, and was walking past the concierge who was talking to someone at the desk when he asked, "Where are you going, Madame?"

"I'm going to the bursar's office."

"Get out of here," he whispered, "the Gestapo's here!"

"Maybe, but we haven't any news from . . . I'd like some news—"

"I've told you, get out!"

That was a close shave! If the concierge hadn't been there, I'd have walked straight into the trap.

I didn't get the information I went there for—the only time that happened—and the other minor problem was there were no return trains before the evening. I had to spend all day there and didn't know anybody. In fact, it's the only day when I could be a tourist. I must have visited every church in Poitiers, and there are plenty of them!

I always memorized my messages; I never, ever had anything written down. But one day, this got me into a real mess. Maurice told me to see Madame Cochet in Chamalières. She was General [Gabriel] Cochet's wife, the former chief of staff of the French Air Force who was in England with de Gaulle. She was to be flown to England in a Lysander [a small aircraft especially used for clandestine missions during World War II]. Maurice told me her address and I thought I had remembered it.

When I arrived in Clermont-Ferrand there was a curfew. I waited until the curfew was over before leaving the station, but unfortunately there was a tramway strike. I had to walk all the way to Chamalières [a mile away]. When I got there, I went to what I thought was the right address. I knocked on the door: "I would like to see Madame Cochet, please." A rather sleepy man answered, "Don't know her."

"But she's expecting me.

"No, she's not here."

Then he asked something that made me think he was in the Resistance as well: "Who sent you?"

"Geneviève."

"No. Not here."

I wandered down the street thinking, It's impossible, I'm sure it's the right house.

In fact I had got it completely wrong! I thought that I had totally messed up the mission. I didn't know what to do. In desperation, I went to sit on a bench, still thinking, What am I going to do?

Suddenly, I saw Madame Cochet leave the hairdresser's, just on the other side of the street! She lived at the beginning of the street while I remembered a number at the end; I've no idea why. I was so relieved. This incident taught me never to forget anything.

This is another example of a mission, one I did with Jacques Hirsch, a Jewish member of the Resistance. I could never have managed to do it alone. We had to transport a direction-finding device for pilots. It was packed into two enormous suitcases and was to be set up in a chimney in a farmhouse. The farmer was supposed to operate the device after hearing a special message on the BBC. It helped pilots find their way when they were flying south.

Jacques Hirsch first had to find the farm and find someone who was willing to do the work—night work. The equipment was dropped by parachute miles away from the farm Jacques had found. Then we took care of transporting it to its destination, always traveling by train. We took a great risk that policemen or soldiers might demand to look inside the cases.

All Jacques's family was involved in the Resistance. They had a daughter and two sons—Pierre, who was Maurice's second radio operator, and Jacques, with whom I often worked during the clandestine period. The girl was also in the network; she was an occasional courier for Maurice.

An apartment rented by Jacques's parents in Toulouse was my base when I was there. His parents ran a ready-to-wear clothes shop in Paris. They took refuge in a small village called Saint-Sulpice-les-Champs. Sometimes we also stayed there. They also lent us money. Maurice would have a prearranged message broadcast by the BBC, which guaranteed they would be reimbursed after the war.

Jacques was an incredibly anxious man. I always admired him for his bravery, because his fear didn't stop him doing the job. To start with, he was rejected by the army because he was Jewish, then he went to study Roman law at Toulouse University. In his final exam he got 19.5 out of 20. He had an extraordinary memory; he read the train timetables so many times for our work that he knew the official railway timetable by heart.

One day Maurice said to me, "Some parachutists have just arrived. They have money for the network; go and collect it.

Go to La Châtre. There's no password; we don't know anybody there and nobody knows you. Just in case there's a problem, you can say that Robert sent you. Sort it out."

I arrived at the address he had given me in La Châtre—it was a grocer's shop and bistro. There was a lady behind the counter. I said, "Good morning, is Monsieur Langlois in?"

"No, my husband's away today."

"I really need to see him. Money has arrived on behalf of Robert. I've come to collect it for our network."

"Well he's not here. I don't know anything about it."

"Can I come back later?"

"You can come back tomorrow."

"No, I can't come back tomorrow because I have to come by train from Montluçon."

There were only three trains a week, so I couldn't return until the day after.

Two days later, I returned to La Châtre from Montluçon. When I entered the bistro, I saw Madame Langlois's expression and thought, Oh dear, I'm in for trouble. I sensed it immediately.

A man whom I had never seen before entered through a side door. He said, "Good morning, Madame."

"Good morning, Monsieur."

"I'm Robert. I don't know you."

"Indeed, well I don't know you either."

"Follow me."

He led me up a spiral staircase into a room where I noticed a door ajar. He asked me to sit down and started interrogating me. We didn't work for the same network, so he didn't know any of the people I knew and vice versa. After a number of other questions I could not answer, I started to panic. Deep down I was wondering what on earth I was going to do. I didn't want to play my trump card for the sake of the network's security.

Finally, when all other attempts had failed, I said, "Do you know Octave?"

"No."

"Octave is Monsieur Chantraine!"

"Ah, yes."

"I was parachuted to his farm on September 23."

At that moment, four or five chaps came out of the next room. Robert was convinced that I was in Pétain's militia, the Milice [the Milice Française, or French militia, that worked for Vichy France and against the Resistance], and to avoid putting his men at risk, he had everything prepared to pop me off. He wrote about this incident in a magazine published on the Resistance immediately after the war. The magazine was edited in Châteauroux and called *The Bazooka*. He wrote an article explaining that he had planned to strangle me. If I had not managed to convince him with the last name, I don't know how I would have got out of it—I really don't know how. If I hadn't known Chantraine . . . Being killed by another resister, that would have been the end!

I had no personal means of transport, but I used something very practical—an annual rail card. Maurice discovered that it was valid for the set routes we needed to use. It was quite expensive but worthwhile because there were many travelers, very few trains, and long queues [lines] at the ticket offices. You even needed a special ticket for some trains. With the annual rail card you didn't queue and you could get on the trains reserved for travelers with the pass.

I usually traveled at night so I didn't get much sleep, but there weren't as many controls then. For long journeys, such as the one I did quite frequently from Toulouse to Riom, I left at 7 PM and didn't arrive until 11 AM the next morning. Sometimes I would take a "couchette," but only for part of the journey because I had to change trains. I was very surprised when I first used a couchette because men and women were mixed up together in the same compartment. There were four couchettes in a compartment; we slept on the top or the bottom bunk. And this was first class, the way I always traveled.

When I took the train I always had a collection of pro-German magazines in French. There was one called *Signal*, another *Carrefour*—that kind of magazine. Only one person ever spoke to me, because I didn't look French. I looked German, especially as I did my hair in the German style, in a plait around my head.

When I was on the move, I had nowhere to cook and I didn't eat in small bistros but in restaurants that obtained their food from the black market. They were all over France and anyone could go if you had the right introduction—but it was also dangerous, for you never knew who would be inside.

When I was in Clermont-Ferrand I ate at the Brasserie de Strasbourg where all the extras were black market–supplied. Food in France was scarce, but we agents were always supplied with enough money to live—and eat—decently. The French gendarmerie [regular French police] controlled the black market. Some were accomplices and closed their eyes to certain things. However, when they went to Gare Montparnasse in Paris, to control the black market, that was another story! These gendarmes would seize black market products for themselves.

A lot of people went to Villedieu-les-Poêles in Normandy to get food. It was obvious what the travelers getting off the trains were up to. They all had such big suitcases they had to drag them along—you could almost see the blood from the meat dripping out. An enormous number of gendarmes would wait for these trains from Normandy. They would let two or three people go by; then they would stop one. They would ask what was in the case and the people had no choice, they had to open it. So they were fined and the goods were confiscated.

My false identity when I was working for Maurice was Marie Jeanne Marthe Vergès, who was someone else's real identity. Jacques Hirsch had taken me to a village called Montaut-les-Créneaux. The local mayor showed me the births and deaths register and told me to choose a name. Marie Jeanne Marthe Vergès was slightly older than me. She had completely disappeared. It was a real identity, but nobody knew what had happened to the girl.

My cover was this: I was posing as a representative for Isabelle Lancray, a cosmetics firm that my future father-in-law had established with a partner. I had official papers and everything I needed. I don't need to add that I didn't have time to do much selling! The cover story was mainly for all the traveling and identity controls. You had to be able to answer the first basic questions. It also helped me to rent the room in Montluçon. I left publicity brochures in the room and the landlady saw me coming and going at completely irregular hours but she thought I was a representative.

On only one occasion did I have the impression that someone suspected that I was not really a cosmetics representative. It was just before D-day, during my last train journey from Montluçon to Paris. The journey had been an absolute nightmare because on top of the usual problems, many train lines had been blown up. I had spent all night changing trains. Toward the end of the journey, when we were near Paris, I was sitting on top of the toilet in the water closet as there was nowhere else to sit. I was sleepy, the train was overcrowded; it was dreadful. A man had been watching me for quite a while and without warning he said, "What do you do for a living?"

"I'm a representative for beauty products."

"Well it doesn't look like it; you're not wearing any makeup this morning."

"Do you think I feel like putting makeup on after the night I've just spent?"

I'm sure he suspected something strange about me. But I actually never wore any makeup and, apart from that one incident, I was never questioned about it.

Until D-day, we didn't need the whole French population with us, if only for security reasons. The smaller and tighter the network, the better. Ours covered a territory which, in my opinion, was far too wide [between Paris, Vierzon, Châteauroux, Montluçon, Clermont-Ferrand, Limoges, Toulouse, Tarbes, and Poitiers.]

Our liaison missions forced us to be continually on the move. It took a huge amount of time. I have no idea what Jacqueline Nearne did; she arrived before me and was Maurice's other courier. I have absolutely no idea, even though she was there for over a year.

Our work consisted of forming small groups all over the place, so that on D-day the groups could expand and help the Allies. That's what happened in the north of Indre and the Cher valley.

7

THE MICHELIN
FACTORY AFFAIR

After the French government surrendered to Germany, many French factory owners began to work for the Germans at the request of the Vichy government—some of them eagerly, some of them begrudgingly (see note on page 166). Many did it because it meant their employees could stay in France rather than being forced to work in Germany. But regardless of what motivated the owners to collaborate with the Germans, their factories—many of which produced materials and goods for the German war machine—were a frequent target of SOE sabotage.

Sabotage was usually more effective and less costly in terms of civilian loss of life than the alternative, which was bombing by the RAF. Additional and unnecessary destruction of nonessential elements of the factory was prevented as well: sabotage raids could precisely target only the key working elements of the factory. For these reasons, many owners of French factories working for the German war machine reluctantly agreed to cooperate with the Resistance by allowing their factories to be sabotaged rather than bombed by the RAF.

Pearl's initial work in occupied France took place in the large region of Auvergne, the site of the Michelin works, an enormous factory in the city of Clermont-Ferrand that was manufacturing tires for the Germans. While in Auvergne, Pearl attempted to assist the Resistance leaders there on behalf of Stationer, offering to help train them in the use of weapons and explosives. In the following account, she explains why she was prevented from doing so.

Before he went on leave in October 1943, Maurice Southgate had gone to see the Michelin factory's service manager, suggesting that he cooperate with the Auvergne resistance efforts to sabotage his factory or else the RAF would bomb it. The manager refused to believe that the RAF would have the time to attack the factory, and so it was left to the untrained Auvergne sabotage team to prevent an RAF raid on the area.

Maurice Southgate went on leave just before the winter of '43–'44—the long, hard winter when no parachute drop was possible for three months. It was then I was involved in the Michelin affair. The Michelin works was located in Clermont-Ferrand, which was surrounded by vineyards. When I first arrived in September 1943 most of my work was in Clermont-Ferrand, an area that had previously been unfamiliar to me. The vines had changed color—they were red, yellow, and so on. It was beautiful, really magnificent. I stayed in the house of the former director of the École des Beaux-Arts at Clermont-Ferrand, Monsieur Dezandes. He had resigned from his position because he wouldn't follow Pétain. Monsieur and Madame Dezandes were extraordinary people who have never been mentioned or written about. I stayed with them for three weeks until my luggage was retrieved and on several later occasions.

Monsieur and Madame Dezandes took an enormous risk lodging SOE agents. To us their house was a peaceful haven; we were much more relaxed there. Madame Dezandes welcomed us with open arms. And you know, even though the house was freezing cold because they didn't have any way of heating it, she always managed to feed us.

We usually tried to eat elsewhere, but sometimes, well, it wasn't always possible. We had breakfast there, which wasn't as easy as it sounds, because there was no tea, coffee, or drinking chocolate, and definitely no milk. We drank grilled barley instead of coffee.

The only relaxing times we had were in the homes where we stayed. We trusted our hosts completely. For security reasons we didn't mention our work; our conversations were commonplace. Their help was priceless.

There wasn't much I could do during those three weeks while waiting for my luggage, but during that time Maurice introduced me to the young courier for the Auvergne network. Something quite funny happened when we met. I'm sure Maurice did it on purpose. He must have told him, "Tomorrow morning we have a meeting with an agent who has just arrived." We met in a park in Clermont-Ferrand. You should have seen his expression when he saw me! At that moment I didn't understand why. Later, when I was wondering why he had looked so surprised to see me there, the penny dropped— he must have been expecting a man, not a woman! I had a lot to do with him later because, during the clandestine period, I worked a lot in Auvergne.

One day [while Maurice Southgate was on leave during the fall of 1943], our radio operator, Amédée Maingard, gave us a message from London. It was an ultimatum: "Blow up the Michelin factory or we shall bomb it!" The Michelin factory was manufacturing tires for the Germans. I thought, No, it was impossible to bomb the factory; it was in Clermont, surrounded by houses. So I contacted Monsieur [Henri] Ingrand [whom Pearl had met before], the head of the resistance in the Auvergne region, and said, "We have an ultimatum, what do you want to do about it?"

During my first chat with Monsieur Ingrand, I had asked him, "How do you learn to use the arms and explosives sent to you?" and he replied, "By our mistakes." I was so horrified I asked if he wanted me to teach his sabotage team. I added something that crossed my mind at the last moment: "But if they don't want a woman, I can send someone else." I was thinking of Amédée. The answer was, "They don't want a woman." I discovered that Gaspard from Auvergne—Monsieur Coulaudon, who led the sabotage team in the Auvergne Maquis—was antiwomen.

The contact with Auvergne was eventually lost because just at that time [just before time had run out on the ultimatum] I became ill. I had intercostal neuralgia [a condition involving severe pain in the nerves between the ribs]—I couldn't move. I sent Henri to Auvergne to try to maintain the contact with the sabotage team. He spent all night standing up in a train to travel from Paris to the little station in Auvergne, where I had planned a meeting with the saboteurs. But as they didn't know Henri, they were very wary of him, ignoring him so much that he had trouble finding anything to eat in the village. So he couldn't organize any training and Michelin was bombed after Gaspard's team failed three times to sabotage the factory. Michelin had a sprinkler system and the first attempt just flooded the place.

The British bombs fell exactly where they had to. I learned later that one of Michelin's sons was in England and he told them precisely where the bombs had to explode. We had outstanding pilots for that sort of bombing in England. They dropped them right on target.

I also learned later that the Michelin owners had been to Madrid to see our military attaché, to reach an agreement to avoid being bombed. They proposed sabotaging the supplies when they left the factory so the owners wouldn't lose as much money. But this isn't something to spread around, because a book has been written about the Resistance in Auvergne and the story isn't quite the same!

A few years ago I took part in a seminar in Clermont-Ferrand, and I spoke about the Dezandes family. Obviously nobody had heard of them, except for one man whom I saw again the next day. He was very pleased to hear me talk about the Dezandes, because he knew what they had done. I asked him, "As for your Monsieur Gaspard and the Michelin factory [the failed sabotage attempts], nobody talks about them?" He wasn't too happy! Which just goes to prove not everything was successful; it's human to make mistakes.

8

ARREST OF A RESISTANCE LEADER

Shortly before he was arrested, Maurice Southgate had sent a report to the SOE offices in London explaining that he considered the first week in the field the most dangerous for an agent because of nerves and unfamiliarity with the new area. Then, after six months, an agent tended to become complacent about security procedures, and if they became ill or exhausted, disaster would most likely follow.

On May 1, 1944, Maurice Southgate, an excellent but exhausted leader who had been working in France for nearly one and a half years, failed to notice clear signs of danger outside a home where members of the Stationer network had been staying in Montluçon. Maurice had planned to meet his radio operator in order to read some messages. When he opened the door, he was faced with the guns of multiple Gestapo agents. They arrested him because he couldn't give them a good explanation as to why he was visiting a house where they had just discovered three radio sets, radio messages, and a huge pile of cash.

Pearl had planned a picnic for that same day and pressured some members of the exhausted team to join her, not realizing that this gesture would have a drastic impact on their destinies.

Henri could feel trouble brewing. He had arrived from Paris the evening before—the night of April 30–May 1, 1944—to the Lhospitaliers' house [the home where Robert Lhospitalier, a member of the Stationer network, lived with his wife and his grandmother] in rue de Rimard. We all sensed D-day was about to happen.

That night Maurice went to meet John Farmer and Nancy (Wake) Fiocca, a team parachuted to join the Auvergne Maquis. On his return from this meeting, where he had received information and money, he was arrested. He forgot to look behind him when he arrived at the Lhospitaliers', because he was very tired. He explained this to me when he returned from Buchenwald concentration camp. There was a front-wheel-drive Citroën, the car used mainly by the Gestapo, hidden further down the street. "If I had seen it, I wouldn't have rung the bell," he told me.

The Gestapo was there. They were looking for Robert Lhospitalier, as he had refused to do his STO, the German compulsory work service. Maurice rang. It was too late for him. Luckily for us, Robert Lhospitalier's grandmother was ill and had called the doctor. When the doctor arrived the Germans refused to let him in. But he insisted on seeing his patient and he managed to enter. The grandmother took advantage of his visit to give him a note, "The Gestapo are in the house," and she jotted down the address of Robert's parents-in-law in rue Bienassis.

We just missed being caught. We weren't in the house when the Gestapo arrived. Why had I suggested a picnic that day? Why had I insisted that our radio operator, Amédée Maingard, come with us? It must be fate.

With the grandmother's note, the doctor warned the family-in-law—Monsieur and Madame Bidet—who knew we were picnicking. When we saw Monsieur Bidet, as white as a sheet, arrive on his bike, we all stood up together. He said, "The Gestapo's at Rimard [referring to the street where the Lhospitalier home was located]."

The Germans took Maurice and [Sergeant René] Mathieu, the young, newly arrived radio operator, who was staying with Robert's mother and grandmother. They took them to Montluçon prison. Robert's mother ended up in prison in Moulins, but she wasn't deported—one of the few. We never saw Mathieu again. His name is on the SOE memorial at Valençay.

When the Germans saw the radio, the money, the list of landing spots for parachute drops, they must have thought there were other people in the network. They encircled the town the next day.

The evening Maurice was arrested, Henri and Jacques Hirsch slept in a bistro on a billiard table. I was in a rented room in rue Chantoiseau. The next day when we discussed what we were going to do, we saw the barricade on the bridge and lots of Germans in lorries [trucks]. Luckily, Jacques Hirsch met someone he knew in Montluçon. He asked him if he could get us out of town. He took us in his car along a small road. We traveled to Saint-Gaultier to warn our other radio operator and asked him to send the message to be broadcast by the BBC, "Hector is very ill." This meant Maurice had been arrested. Such messages were broadcast to warn members of our network.

Then he dropped us off near Néris-les-Bains (Allier) and we took a taxi to the crossroads of Dun-le-Poëlier, in Indre. Henri and I walked the rest of the way to Les Souches, to Monsieur and Madame Sabassier, while Jacques Hirsch went to Châteauroux. Amédée Maingard and Robert Lhospitalier had both gone in different directions without saying where, for security reasons.

Maurice was taken to the Gestapo on avenue Foch in Paris. To start with, nobody knew who he was. The Germans had no idea what he did until his photograph was shown to someone he knew. They asked the person, "Do you know this man?" and he replied, "Yes, it's Maurice Southgate." At least a month went by between his arrest on May 1, 1944, and his arrival at the Gestapo.

When the Gestapo found out that it was Maurice Southgate—who, after all, was someone quite important—he was forced to "give" information concerning the network. He probably gave the sector Dun-le-Poëlier where, apart from Alex [head of the local communist FTP; his real name was Briant], nothing was organized. That must be why we started having trouble when the Germans came a month later at the beginning of June—Monsieur [Armand] Mardon, the mayor of Dun-le-Poëlier and regional councilor, was arrested. It's not certain but very likely.

Maurice was taken to Buchenwald concentration camp. He was one of 36 English agents deported to that camp. Out of 36, only 4 survived; all the others were hanged. The survivors had taken the identity of someone who had already died, with the complicity of [Dr. Alfred] Balachowski, the French head of the infirmary.

Maurice told me all this the day after he returned to England. First they hanged 15, then another 15, and finally 2. Nobody knows why. And do you know how they did it? With butchers' hooks through the base of their skulls.

When he came back he looked appalling: completely shaved head, blank stare, gaunt. He neither wanted to talk nor hear about the war.

THE BATTLE OF LES SOUCHES

On the afternoon of June 5, 1944, the SOE offices in London got word that D-day, the long hoped-for Allied invasion of German-occupied France on the coast of Normandy, was finally going to occur on the following day. Coded orders were sent over the BBC that evening to agents, resisters, and Maquis in occupied France to engage in sabotage that would immediately impede the German rush to the Normandy coast.

On June 11, 1944, at eight o'clock in the morning, 2,000 Germans attacked Pearl's band of 20 Maquis along with the neighboring Communist band under the command of Alex. The Germans obviously thought there were more Maquis in Pearl's area, which is why they sent so many fighting men there. Among other things, their mistake highlights the fierce combat strength of the Maquis.

The Maquis weren't supposed to fight all-out until D-day, but these French fighters had been harassing

German troops by attempting to diminish their ranks, lower their morale, and hinder their movements to some extent all throughout the occupation. The Battle of Les Souches was partly German retaliation against the Maquis in that area as well as an attempt to stifle the sudden and relentless sabotage efforts against the attempted German defense of the Normandy landings.

We reached north Indre on May 2, 1944, just after Maurice's arrest in Montluçon. We were based on an estate, Les Souches, and lodged in the guardhouse of the château where Monsieur and Madame Sabassier lived with their daughter, Yvonne. From May 1 to June 11, I went on two more missions, and some arms were parachuted. Madame Sabassier prepared our meals, while we cycled around getting the contacts we needed.

Immediately after D-day, Henri commandeered all the château's outbuildings for the Resistance. The château's owners, Monsieur and Madame Hay des Nétumières, had little idea of what was happening. On June 11 we told them to escape, but they just wouldn't listen. They said they weren't running any risks because they supported Pétain. They were arrested. Monsieur Hay des Nétumières was killed near Blois by [Pierre] Paoli, a Frenchman working for the Gestapo [who hunted down Jews and resisters in central France]. Madame Hay des Nétumières died at Ravensbrück [a concentration camp for women].

A few days after D-day a man arrived at Les Souches by bicycle. The men at the guard post at the end of the lane, on the main road, stopped him and brought him to me. When I asked him where he had come from he said from Paris. I asked him if he had seen barricades en route, and when he said no, I was flabbergasted. It meant that none of the networks between Paris and Les Souches had obeyed London's orders to block the roads. We were the only ones to have done so, by felling trees across the main road. I immediately thought, Heavens, we're the bridge-head.

Sure enough, two or three days later we were attacked. The snooper plane had spotted the trees we had felled. For a time, the Germans used the snooper, a small plane they flew to examine the land if they didn't know it very well. They must have concluded there were quite a number of us hiding in the Taille de Ruine woods. I have never understood why ours was the only team to have obeyed orders.

My lieutenant, Raymond Billard, or "Gaspard," a discharged sailor and member of the Wrestler circuit, told me that the day after the snooper had flown over, he and four others were driving in a Citroën front-wheel drive from the château to Monsieur Sabassier's house when they came face-to-face with the Germans. Both parties were very surprised to see each other! The Germans got out and machine-gunned them, but none of them were hurt.

When more German soldiers appeared, the lads on the main road blew the bugle—but obviously not loudly enough. It was our danger signal but I was the only person to hear it. I told Henri, "We're under attack." He replied, "No, it's Sunday, we can't be attacked on a Sunday." Father Valuche was celebrating mass nearby in the château. Monsieur Sabassier and the rest of us tried to see who was coming, but it was a long way; we couldn't see very well. Then Henri had an idea: "We'll fire into the air and we'll know straightaway if they're Germans or other Maquis members." Sure enough, we found out immediately.

I threw on my clothes, picked up my bag and the cocoa tin where the money was kept. As I climbed down the ladder from the attic, German bullets were whizzing past my ears. At the bottom, I jumped on my bike and cycled to the château's out-houses where the weapons we had just received were stocked. They hadn't even been cleaned yet and were still covered in pro-tective grease. I hastily loaded the guns anyway and put detona-tors in the hand grenades.

Then one of the chaps rushed up to me and told me to leave as quickly as possible: the Germans were approaching. They had got out of their trucks and were advancing in extended order across the plain toward the château. I dropped everything and ran to La Barraque, a farm that was about a mile from the château. Henri was hiding; he saw two Germans coming along a path. He shot at them, killed one, and retreated.

I didn't want to be caught in a house. I fled into a wheat field. Almost immediately I saw flames shooting out of the barn. The Germans had set fire to it in retaliation. I lay down, very scared lest the wheat should catch fire. I was hoping to reach the under-wood [underbrush] when they saw me and started shooting, but I wasn't hit. I crawled across the field on my hands and knees, only moving when the wind blew and stirred the crops. I was awfully hot and frightened in the blazing sun.

I had a revolver. I decided that if arrested it would be bet-ter if I weren't carrying any weapons, so I buried it. In fact it was never found. All day long I remained hidden in the field. I couldn't leave it because German lorries were constantly com-ing and going—Henri counted 56—also the field was out in the open. There was a moment when the German snooper plane flew over, so I curled up in a ball hoping they would think I was just a bag or something.

I was still lying in the field at about 10:30 PM. I could no longer hear the lorries. I looked up and saw the farmer's wife putting out the fire. I stood up and waved, but Madame Sabassier and her daughter, Yvonne, were so frightened when they saw me on the other side of the wheat field, they rushed back indoors. They didn't recognize me because it was dark and because they'd had an extremely tense day. I went to join them. They hadn't much food to give me because they had been feeding the Germans all day. They managed to find two eggs, which I ate, and then I made my way to the Trochets' house.

They had tried to join Henri and Monsier Sabassier, who were hidden together in a wheat field, but they couldn't make it all the way across the courtyard before the Germans arrived and started shooting at them from all angles. They would have been killed in the courtyard. So they returned to the house with the farmer's wife and her maid.

The Germans followed the women, ordered them outside, pointed their guns at them, and demanded to know where the "terrorists" were. The women didn't know, so they couldn't tell them anything. So the Germans kept the four women covered all day and forced them to cook. Madame Sabassier made them omelettes that the women had to taste before the Germans would eat them.

The women considered themselves lucky because these Germans were middle-aged Wehrmacht [regular German army] men, not SS. They sensed the war was nearly over and were content to stay inside the house since they didn't know how many Maquis were in the area or how well they were armed. One of them spoke French. He had a conversation with Madame Sabassier, whose son was in Germany. He said, "The war's a bad thing. I come from Russia."

In the afternoon, the Germans captured the neighboring farmer's son, Roger Catineau, whose knee was injured. He had managed to bury his gun and had hidden in a thicket not far from La Barraque. When they found him they were angry. To make things worse, they found some hand grenades in a stock of firewood. They set fire to them and they exploded all over the place; the whole cowshed burned down. As the fire spread, the farmer let out the cows and horses, which created bedlam in the courtyard. The Germans asked for *eau de vie* [distilled alcohol], and they wiped Catineau's knee with it. They took him with them but released him in Orleans, near a drug store.

In the evening, they said to the women, "We're taking the four of you with us." They made them climb into the lorry, but another order was given and they were told to get out again. They were lucky not to have been deported. The Germans left the same evening.

Henri, Monsieur Sabassier, and Monsieur Baron had spent the day in hiding watching over the house. They had decided that if the Germans did anything to the women, they would attack. It wasn't necessary because these Germans didn't feel like fighting anymore; they were quite happy where they were.

The day had been hectic, but it wasn't over yet for me. I borrowed a bike to go to the farm called Doulçay [Maray]. I got lost on the way. I knew I had to turn right at a certain crossroads where there was a cross. I finally found the cross—I hadn't realized it was so far—and I turned right; then I heard someone talking. It was dark so I couldn't see very well. I assumed it was one of the men on guard, but no, it was a man all by himself. He said to me, "So you'se a woman then . . . "

"Yes, I'm a woman."

Then he lurched forward to kiss me! Well, I really didn't fancy being kissed by him. It was a chap I knew of from Maray who drank rather a lot and wandered about by himself at night. What a great way to end such a day!

Next morning, the priest from Anjouin came to tell the Sebassiers where they could find their father. Yvonne and Madame

Sabassier walked back to Les Souches to try to find the grandmother. The Germans had left her in the middle of a manure heap, but they hadn't hurt her. She was taken in by Monsieur Barboux of Les Léoments farm. They brought her home the following Monday.

The Sabassiers' house in Les Souches had been completely wrecked. The Germans had destroyed all the furniture by shooting holes in it. The only thing they could retrieve, to begin with, was some linen. They decided to come back the next day, Tuesday, with Monsieur Barboux, his car, and horse to salvage as much as possible. But at 7 AM Tuesday the Germans burned their house. They realized what was happening before they got there because they heard the incendiary grenades exploding. The Sabassiers later learned that the Germans had returned with the Gestapo to arrest them because of the pile of stuff they had found—weapons, a radio set, and so on.

The battle of Les Souches wasn't just a skirmish. It was a planned attack by Germans against what they assumed to be a large Maquis group. I later learned we had been attacked by three German garrisons who had encircled the whole Dun-le-Poëlier sector. Les Souches was just a small part of a larger battle in which 32 French people lost their lives.

10

ORGANIZING THE MAQUIS

After the arrest of Maurice Southgate, Stationer's radio operator and assistant organizer, Amédée Maingard, and Pearl split the enormous Stationer network into three sections. Pearl took the northern part of the Indre department, which she renamed Marie-Wrestler circuit after two of her code names. It is believed that, at this point in time, Pearl's image was placed on German "wanted" posters (see note on page 167) in the Montluçon area with a large monetary award offered for her arrest.

While initiating her second wave of Resistance work immediately following the Battle of Les Souches, Pearl stayed with the Trochet family, Monsieur and Madame Henri Trochet—whom Pearl affectionately referred to as Grandpa and Grandma Trochet—and their son. Then, while still taking her meals with the Trochets, she lived in the woods with Henri—who worked under Pearl as her second in command—and the men of the Maquis, who knew her by the code name "Pauline" (the name of one of Pearl's childhood dolls). Immediately after D-day, realizing that the Allies now had a good chance of winning the war, there was a flood of volunteers who joined whatever Maquis groups they could find—especially those with leaders who could, like Pearl, keep them supplied with weapons.

Although during training in London Pearl had expressed alarm at the idea of liaising with a leader who controlled a 1,000-strong Maquis group, she soon became the leader of an even larger group herself. Shortly after D-day, the Marie-Wrestler circuit prevented numerous German troops and munitions from reaching the Normandy coast by staging constant acts of railroad sabotage. At one point, Pearl passed on to London information that led to the RAF bombing of a German train of 60 tanks of gasoline that had been headed for Normandy. The destruction of the tanks delayed numerous German troops from reaching the coast.

From June 12, we stayed at Doulçay, a farm near Maray, with Monsieur and Madame Henri Trochet and their son André. Madame Trochet cooked and we had a room overlooking the back of the farm. Farms had rather rudimentary comfort in those days: you had to use a pitcher to wash and there was no loo [toilet]. When we had nothing to do we helped Monsieur Trochet harvest crops because it was summer. But we were not very good at it; we were very amateurish farmers.

Grandma Trochet hardly ever talked and was always very gentle, but she knew exactly what she was up to. She managed the farm with skill and without making a fuss about it. But

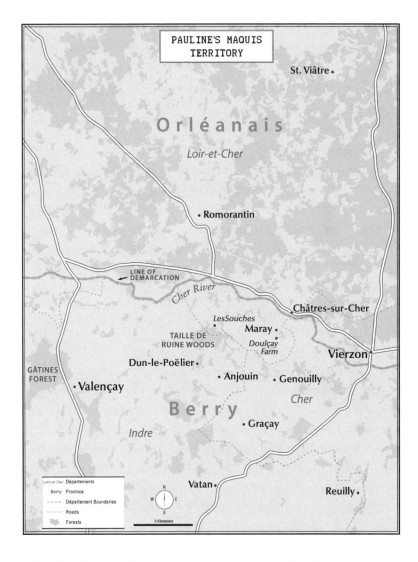

Monsieur Trochet had a very strong personality. He was a typical man of Berry. He had an enormous moustache and always had a hat screwed onto his head. Maybe he had a cold tummy because he always wore a cummerbund over his trousers. He loved hunting and fishing, so it was actually his wife, Madame

Trochet, who worked the farm. She took care of the animals and everything to do with the house. Grandpa Trochet did all the heavy work outside. They had 250 acres in all, some crops, some woodland, there was a large vegetable garden, about 20 cows, goats, chickens, and Muscovy ducks.

One day his car wouldn't start so Monsieur Trochet took me to Mennetou station with the neighbor's horse and cart. And you don't have to believe me, but the horse stopped all on his own in front of the bistro before reaching the station. When I asked Grandpa Trochet if he was going to visit us in Paris, he didn't want to. He replied "I'm not goin' there, you'se only drink water."

He didn't even use much water to wash himself—it was done so quickly. One day he had something wrong with his teeth, I don't know what. There was a dentist in the Maquis, he broke a drill on Grandpa's teeth they were so hard. He used a finger to brush his teeth, once to the right, once to the left—all brushed. It was the same for everything he did. All right, I'll wash, but is it really necessary?

He had an amazing sense of humor and a sensational way of telling stories with his accent. I can't imitate him. He also cheated a bit at cards. One day I saw his wife playing with him. I whispered to her, "Be careful when you play, he cheats." She replied, "Yes, me too, but he doesn't know it." They were an amazing couple.

The Battle of Les Souches left us in a hopeless state—we had nothing left, no weapons and no radio. The Krauts had pinched everything except the money I had hidden under my bed in a cocoa tin. I managed to take it with me when we were attacked. If I remember rightly we had about 500,000 francs [see note on page 168]. In any case it was a large amount because it lasted for a long time. Because we had no radio, the only way I could contact London for more supplies to be parachuted was by going to

Saint-Viâtre on the other side of the demarcation line across the Cher River, to meet Philippe de Vomécourt [known by his SOE code name, "Saint Paul"], who could send a message via radio. Pierre Chassagne, a former member of the Adolphe subnetwork, knew where I could find someone in Saint-Viâtre who could help me get in touch with Saint Paul. Around June 14, Pierre came to Doulçay and we cycled north to Saint-Loup to cross the Cher. I took off my shoes, carried my bike on my shoulders, and waded across over some damned sharp stones.

Shortly after we had arrived in Saint-Viâtre we decided it was time to have lunch. We stopped on a bank along the side of the road to eat our sandwiches—Madame Trochet must have made them. Then I noticed a front-wheel-drive vehicle coming from the left toward us; the engine made a very characteristic, familiar noise. I recognized the registration number; it was Monsieur Hay des Nétumières's car with Germans inside. I said to Chassagne, "Now it's Saint Paul's turn to be attacked."

He left me sitting on the bank and went into Saint-Viâtre to make contact. When he reached his contact, he was told the Germans had come to attack Saint Paul's Maquis. But the Maquis had dispersed just in time. The car we had seen was probably carrying officers leading the way for the trucks of soldiers. But our trip to Saint-Viâtre was a waste of time because I still had no way of contacting London.

Two days later, Chassagne came to me and said, "I'll go alone, give me the message." I gave him the message, which he hid in the bike's saddle support. After Saint Paul had received it, he came to visit me in Doulçay disguised, as usual, as a gamekeeper. He said Germans always respected uniforms. And he was so well disguised that I didn't recognize him at first!

He had transmitted my message to London, and on June 24 we received a large parachute drop on a piece of land we called "whale"—all our landing sites had the names of fish or marine animals. The equipment was parachuted next to Grandmont farm, near the Trochets, on Monsieur Hennequart's land. Three planes were used to carry the supplies—we needed to be completely rearmed.

We received hand grenades, Stens [machine guns], plastic explosives, and so on. Usually when drops were taking place, there weren't many people around for security reasons—we had to avoid going to and fro across the countryside. But this drop was an exception. It was our first big drop after D-day and we spent two days and one night just distributing arms to the Maquis leaders in our sector. I didn't even have time to wash during those two days.

When we were re-equipped we contacted or recontacted everyone willing to help us—in Genouilly, Vatan, Graçay, Dun-le-Poëlier. I often met Alex, the local FTP leader, and spent nearly all my time liaising with the different resistance groups.

Immediately after the Battle of Le Souches we had 20 Maquis at most working with the Stationer network. Now volunteers came flooding in: locals, boys from youth camps, and a few who had been commandeered for the STO [Service du travail obligatoire, the compulsory work service, still operating in 1944] who didn't want to go to Germany and so joined the Maquis.

The men's motivation was to chuck the Germans out. Full stop. Very few of them were married; they were mainly youngsters who were old enough to do their military service. These boys didn't want to join the Communist Maquis, so they came to us. They had learned that we could supply arms.

Within a very short time there were at least 150 of us, and soon after that there were about 1,500. At the end we had about 3,500 men. You can't imagine how much humility I learned from those men. We were dealing with the most down-to-earth farm workers, but there was also an intellectual elite.

One day I said to Henri, "We can't carry on like this; a large group such as this needs to be organized." So we divided them into four Maquis groups: each one had a leader and its own territory. It was an exceptional situation because I, who had worked as a courier, organized them and had the idea of dividing the Nord-Indre Maquis [north Indre, the Marie-Wrestler network] into four subsections.

The first subsection was led by "Comte" [Roland Pérot]; the second by "Parrain" [real name not known] at first, then by "Robert" [Camille Boiziau]; the third by Georges Prieur then by "Emile" [Emile Goumain]; and the fourth by "La Lingerie" [Paul Vannier]—we gave him this name because had an underwear manufacturing business in Reuilly.

The main thing was to stop the Maquis from becoming a completely disorganized shambles. I was in charge, but it was not easy for me because I hadn't been trained for this role. In practice the four subdivisions operated very well and were well supplied. In all, 150 tons of arms were parachuted by 60 planes. The Amicale [group of former resisters from the Norde-Indre and Cher Valley Maquis] still consider me as their leader but only because I was in a very special position when the four sections were formed. In other words, we started organizing these Maquis, we had set it up.

But finally, on July 25, after I had asked repeatedly for a military commander, to my great relief one arrived. He was an army captain called Francis Perdriset. Until then Perdriset and his wife and daughter lived in Châteauroux [the capital of Indre, where the regional leaders of the AS and the FFI had secret headquarters]. He worked near Le Blanc for the Resistance and had been a Maquis instructor long before D-Day.

But when he came to us he wanted to allocate ranks to the
maquisards: sergeant, adjutant, and so on. He was an officer
in the French army and immediately wanted to organize us
as such. I said, "Look, they're all volunteers. I'm not sure it's a
good idea giving them ranks as if they were in an army. There
are four subsectors, each with a leader. It's up to each leader to
decide how to organize his Maquis."

We couldn't act as an army: get up at a fixed time, do a certain
thing, clean the courtyard. Absolutely nothing could be planned
in advance. However, we continued to cooperate with Francis,
and he didn't change the organization of the four Maquis groups.
Each military commander gave instructions to the men. I don't
know exactly what they did as I was never mixed up in this.
The Maquis role was to harass German troops; they fought the
Germans who were passing through the area. There were at
least four, five, or six battles—or rather skirmishes—with the
Germans. I don't know exactly how many. That was their job,
not mine. I let them get on with it; they didn't report to me.

I was in touch with London via our radio operator, request-
ing arms and money for all the Maquis groups we now regularly
visited. I did what I could to keep them all supplied while ensur-
ing we didn't order too many, but though I had this key position
I tried to keep a low profile. One of the *maquisards* wrote a poem
and called me "L'Arlésienne" of the Maquis because I could
never be seen [*L'Arlésienne* is the name of a famous French play
where the title character never appears]. One thing that really
makes my blood boil is hearing people say, "She was in the war,
bang-bang-bang, she blew up trains and all sorts . . ." It's just not
true. All I did was to visit and arm the resisters.

The D-day landing was the turning point in our work. For a
start, there was no more Gestapo, at least in the region where I
was based at the time—the north of Indre and the Cher Valley.

Pearl (far right) and her sisters with Lucy, a World War I Belgian refugee who lived for a time with the family, circa 1919.

Pearl, circa 1926.

above: Pearl (first row, fifth from left) with her troop of Girl Guides (English Girl Scouts), circa 1924.

left: Pearl (far left) with her mother and sisters, circa 1927.

Pearl, circa 1932.

Pearl and her sisters, all dressed
in their WAAF uniforms, before
Pearl left for France in 1943.

Pearl in her WAAF uniform before
she left for France in 1943.

Henri (standing,
fourth from left)
with several of
the other French
POWs at Steinfel
D Stalag XII B,
May 1941. A
German guard on
the far right.

Pearl, circa 1944.

right: Pearl's railway pass that she used while working as a courier and that identified her as Marie Vergès.

below: Pearl's false birth certificate.

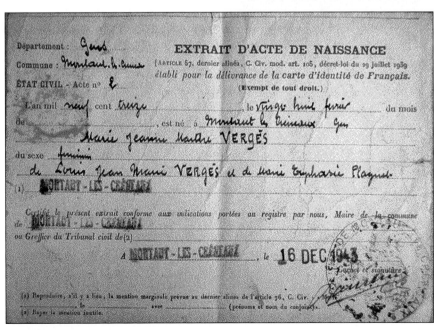

Henri's false ID card identifying him as Jean Gauthier, a farmer.

Les Souches château after the war, as the Germans left it. They returned to the area two days after the Battle of Les Souches and burned much of the estate, including the château.

In Valençay, 1944, after France was liberated. Left to right: the Duke of Valençay (who owned the château where Pearl and Henri stayed when the Maquis were in the Gatines Forest), Princesse Radziwill, Pearl, Francis Perdriset.

With Captain Francis Perdriset leading, Pearl marches in the Liberation of Valençay, France, with the Maquis, September 24, 1944. To her left is Major A. J. Clutton, head of the Jedburgh Team, and to her right is his assistant, J. Vermot ("Broullard").
Courtesy of Daniel Boutineau

Group of resisters in 1944 after France was liberated. Left to right: Jimmy Menzies (the radio operator for the Jedburgh team), Robert Knéper, Henri Cornioley, Francis Perdriset, Roland Perot ("Comte"), Pearl.

Pearl in 1944.

Pearl in 1945.

Henri in 1945.

Pearl and Henri in 1944.

Pearl in New York during the American lecture tour, February 1946. She's pointing to the Marie-Wrestler section of the Stationer network on a map.

Pearl and Henri at the inauguration of a Resistance memorial (the Bruneval Memorial), circa 1947.

Left to right: Pearl; Maurice Buckmaster, head of the SOE's F Section; and Yvonne Cormeau, another agent of the F Section, several decades after the war. They are standing in front of Wanborough Manor, one of the places where SOE agents trained.

At the Trochets' farm near Maray sometime after the war. Henri is on the far left. "Grandpa" Trochet is standing next to Henri wearing a hat. André Trochet, their son, is wearing an open shirt and is standing next to his mother, "Grandma" Trochet. Pearl is standing behind and to the right of Grandma Trochet. Everyone else in the photo is unidentified.

(clockwise from top left)

Pearl when Hervé Larroque interviewed her in 1995.

Pearl during a ceremony in Levroux (Indre), France, May 20, 2004.

Pearl and other former SOE agents standing in front of the SOE memorial in Valençay, France, during a ceremony honoring SOE agents, May 6, 2005. Left to right: Henri Diacono, Jacques Poirier, Pearl, Bob Malouboer.

Pearl with Queen Elizabeth II at the British Embassy in Paris, April 2004, after the queen had awarded Pearl with the CBE (Commander of the British Empire) "for services to UK-French relations and to the history of the Second World War." Upon presenting the award to Pearl, the queen said, "You've waited a long time for this."

The Gestapo and the German army were two completely different things. Secondly, open warfare began. We could fight. It was the period when the Maquis had to prevent the Germans first getting to Normandy and after that, from returning to Germany.

As far as I was concerned working with the Maquis after D-Day was much less tiring and stressful than the clandestine period, when I was working as a courier. I could never have been a spy; it's not in my nature at all! Although I needed a false identity and a false profession, the false cover just enabled me to do my job. To be a secret agent is to be someone else and to have to look for information, sometimes in a completely dishonest way. That's something I'm not comfortable with—acting and doing things on the sly.

I held the purse strings with Henri and Monsieur Gaëtan Ravineau [a member of the Maquis who later became chief treasurer and paymaster]; London didn't send me much money in the beginning, I suspect because I was a woman. Because I was asking for lots of arms at this point they must have deducted that I had a fair-sized team with me, so they sent more money. Some of the lads who joined our Maquis had families to care for, so we had to give them something. Francis Perdriset decided to give them, I think, 20 francs a day each, which wasn't bad in those days. Twenty francs a day for almost two months made quite a tidy sum at the end. The men had to eat, so they had to find a cook, buy food, and so on. Quite a lot of farms supplied food. When necessary, the Maquis requisitioned things: food, bicycles, money, or provisions in exchange for vouchers, which were to be reimbursed after the war.

I had a good relationship with everyone with whom I worked. We were friendly and I never argued with anyone. But then again no one ever questioned what I said—only Alex. I never argued with him, either, but he did his own thing. We were submerged by all the chaps joining us who didn't want to work with him. He was very political; his FTP all wore uniforms with a red star that identified them as Communists.

The first time Philippe de Vomécourt ["Saint Paul"] came to see us in Maray by bicycle, I asked him to visit Alex with me to try and persuade him to remove the stars because if they were captured by the Germans wearing those uniforms, they wouldn't have any chance of coming out alive. It was my caring streak; it was completely idiotic putting human lives at risk out of sheer pride. Philippe de Vomécourt accompanied me to Alex's tent, but it was all in vain. But though the FTP were often in conflict with the Germans, they were never arrested.

His group did their job: guerilla war, destroying railway tracks. Whatever I tried to discuss, all he wanted were arms, arms, and more arms. That's the way it went. I knew I wouldn't be able to do anything with him, but he was in the middle of our sector; we had to put up with him. He had a lot of respect for me, I'm sure of it, but that's all. He never left his tent. He was in the woods and if he needed to see me I had to go to him. He and I also exchanged letters daily. His messenger dropped them in a tree trunk hole. Henri or I went to collect the messages and at the same time left one for him. They were put in a bicycle tire inner tube to protect them from the rain.

Francis [Perdriset] came to live with us in Doulçay, as did Mercier, his assistant who was a lieutenant in the French Air Force. At the time we decided to sleep in the woods. There was a little wood nearby and we set up tents made out of nylon parachutes. To set up the first tent, we attached the top of a parachute to a branch and spread out the cloth. It wasn't bad until it rained, when we realized the inside was full of steam. The drops of water transformed into a sort of drizzle. I said to Henri,

"This isn't very practical; we'll have to put a second parachute over the first, with a gap of about six inches. Maybe the drops will run down the inner one."

We tried it and it worked. We also put up a parachute-tent for Francis and his assistant, one for an office—they had a typewriter—and one for visitors who couldn't make it back to their base. We slept on the ground, on straw supplied by Monsieur Trochet in sleeping bags of a kind, made with more parachutes. We were there until we went to the Gâtines Forest.

Sometimes I'm asked if being surrounded by so many men was difficult for me, but I never had any trouble, or problems with them, never. The men called me "our mother" and they still do. At that time I wasn't old enough to be their mother—I was 29, whereas most of them were about 20—but I was indeed older than them. I suppose they looked on me as an older sister. Also, I had come to help them although I wasn't French; that had something to do with the way they treated me. And everyone knew that Henri and I were together. They always respected us. The first time Grandpa Trochet saw us, he thought, Those two look like they're well and truly together.

During this time girls were often used as couriers. For example Anne and Monique Bled, some couriers I knew, would sometimes cycle all the way from Blois to Valençay. Monique even told me not so long ago that she made that 30-mile trip nearly every day. That takes some cycling. They probably needed weapons near Blois as well, maybe some weapons were sent there. But I do know she came with messages, to see Boiziau, I think. It was all for the benefit of their father, Monsieur Bled, who was in an FTP Maquis near Blois.

As much as possible, she didn't carry written messages. Sometimes, however, she slipped them into the handlebars of her bike or into the satchel, using the paper to wrap up some item or other. But that was rare. She wasn't yet 17 when she told her father she wanted to do this. He would not accept it. Then one day, at the end of December 1943, she said to him, "Listen, you say that we are little girls, but who would be suspicious of little girls? On the contrary, that might be very useful?"

The idea had its way—nobody ever suspected them. One time, though, the Germans stopped her because they wanted her bike. One of them chased her onto a side road, and she said she never had so much courage for pedaling! You understand, he had a grenade in his hand. That reassured her, because she said to herself, If he throws the grenade, he kills the girl, but he doesn't get the bike. You see the little things one depends on! Later she went through some sticky patches and her family was nearly arrested by the Gestapo. She had the same sort of problems as I did with the resistance.

On August 4, when we were still at the Doulçay farm with the Trochets, Comte, who led one of the Maquis, came to find us at the farm to tell us that the evening before he had received a parachuted Jedburgh mission team. Jedburgh teams were composed of three men, including one Frenchman, and were parachuted behind enemy lines after D-day to help groups needing to liaise with England. They were also meant to coordinate the Maquis' actions in order to back the Allies.

When Comte told me about this mission, I said, "What? I don't know anything about this."

"That's why I came to tell you, but we don't know what to do with them. And the three of them are in uniform."

"I must see them because I don't understand what is going on at all."

The next day or the day after, Major A. H. Clutton, an Englishman, arrived at the farm. He was a middle-aged man who had fought at Verdun during the First World War. He was parachuted on August 4 near Vatan along with an English radio operator called T. S. "James" Menzies and a Frenchman called J. Vermot, his assistant, whose code name was "Brouillard" [fog]. I don't know why they decided to send this tall chap in uniform; it was dangerous because there were still Germans about. Anyway I introduced myself by saying, "What are you doing here?"

"And what about yourself?" he replied.

"I'm afraid I've been here quite a while. I'm SOE, I was parachuted in; we have four Maquis groups here."

That's how we met each other.

11

INTO THE FOREST

Except for those who had previously been part of the French armed forces, most Maquis were not and had never been professional soldiers, and the Germans rarely treated them as such. Captured *maquisards* were usually executed immediately rather than being taken prisoner as the Germans would normally do (if they were following the Geneva Conventions) with official members of enemy armed forces. Some of the Maquis' fellow Frenchmen also took issue with their nonprofessional status: the remnants of the French Army—the Armée secrète—and Charles de Gaulle's organization generally, treated the Maquis with only reluctant respect, viewing them as undisciplined and unpredictable bands that needed to be brought under control and made part of the FFI. Charles de Gaulle and his followers especially wanted to control and disarm the Communist Maquis since the size and strength of the French Communist party at that time caused them to fear a postwar Communist takeover of the country.

Although there were some badly run networks and while there was sometimes a general sense of disorganization among Maquis groups, in the main they were effective guerilla fighters who could inflict impressively large casualties on the Germans in rural areas, but only when they were familiar with the terrain in which they were fighting. When the Maquis had leaders who understood how to maximize their potential, they could be trained into an impressive fighting force.

But as the war progressed and the Nazis' grip on France began to weaken, the AS and the FFI began to assert more control over the Maquis. One consequence of this was that all four sections of the Marie-Wrestler Network—approximately 3,500 Maquis—were ordered to move into the Gâtines Forest.

The regional leaders of the AS and the FFI—most of whom had been secretly headquartered at Châteauroux—frustrated the Maquis by deliberately moving them out of familiar territory. But the Americans who arrived on the scene (and who knew almost nothing about the Maquis) infuriated these rural French fighters even more, albeit in a much more innocent but ignorant way, during what became known as the Surrender of the Elster Column.

The Gâtines Forest starts where the SOE memorial is located near Valençay. A large part of the forest belonged to the duke of Valençay. It was there that the F-Section of the SOE began: the first SOE contact in France was with Max Hymans [a French resister] when a radio operator, Frenchman Georges Bégué, was parachuted there on May 6, 1941. This was also where I completed my own SOE work.

Commander "Surcouf" [Colonel Paul Minguet] in Châteauroux was chief of the Secret Army in the Indre department. In fact he wasn't our chief because we never saw him; but as he oversaw Indre, I presume we were under his jurisdiction. We didn't have any other contact with them except for Francis Perdriset's arrival.

Toward the end of August, Francis Perdriset received orders to move all the Maquis to meet up in the Gâtines Forest, near Valençay. The order came from Colonel Minguet in Châteauroux. Everybody had to go, including us. I was furious and I said, "It's completely ridiculous. You can't expect these men to go to an area they don't know to engage the enemy in guerilla warfare; you have to know the land well to do that."

Our greatest strength was knowing our territory. The Maquis could not fight like soldiers, who fire at each other, advance to occupy territory, retreat, and so on. Guerrilla warfare isn't the same; you have to hassle the enemy and retreat immediately. You cannot plan to occupy territory or seek face-to-face combat.

But I wasn't in command, so nothing I said had any weight. I think Colonel Chomel [chief military counselor of the Indre FFI] gave the orders to move there; he was thinking like a military commander, imagining we were soldiers. But I was there to help, so I followed. We took the four Maquis groups [of the Marie-Wrestler network] there, and we stayed in the Gâtines Forest from the end of August to mid-September, with the Gâtines Maquis. According to the statistics, which came out much later, there were 3,500 to 3,700 volunteers scattered inside the forest at that time, whereas I thought there were about 1,500.

When we arrived in Gâtines, we first slept in a farm called Colombier that was in the forest. There was a lot of movement because the courtyard was large [the farm was noisy and busy with Maquis wandering in and out]. Later, in September, when we were sure there weren't too many Germans in the vicinity, we moved into the château in Valençay. We stayed there for a while.

Some of the Louvre's treasures were stored away in the château, including the sculptures Victoire de Samothrace, the Venus de Milo, and engravings by Rembrandt and [Albrecht] Dürer. In one sense, our bedroom was nicely decorated. But it wasn't a bedroom; it seemed to us more of a ballroom. The bed was at least six by six feet, like a battlefield!

The works of art were locked away in cases. Employees from the national museums were there and opened one of them for us. André Leroi-Gourhan [a famous French archaeologist and anthropologist] took that initiative. He said, "I'll show you things the public never sees." He showed us a very old tiara belonging to the pope and engravings by Rembrandt where you could see corrections to the drawing on the copper.

Luckily for us, we were in the Gâtines Forest after the battle of August 16. The Germans did a lot of damage in Valençay that day. I wasn't there, but Francis was. He was told to stand against a wall, he really thought he had had it. The Germans set fire to things, shot, killed. It wasn't as bad as Oradour-sur-Glane [a notorious SS atrocity that took place about 100 miles to the south], but it wasn't a pretty sight. When we were there, only a few Germans passed through our territory. All the Maquis in France, wherever they were, had been told to stop the Germans from returning to Germany.

At the outset Churchill said, "Set Europe ablaze." All they wanted to do was to get rid of the Germans, and for that London gave us the means to do it. But they weren't aware of how we operated. Also, I'm not sure there were two Maquis groups organized—or disorganized—in the exact same way. Every one of us did what we could with whatever means we had at our disposal. Our first objective was to stop the Germans from reaching Normandy and, later, we had to stop them from returning to Germany.

We ended up having two wounded German soldiers with us: a youngster and an officer who was wounded in both legs. They were in an ambushed truck, hit by a bazooka. We took the youngster to the hospital run by nuns in Valençay. The officer, a captain in the German army, was 100 percent pro-Hitler and had decided he wanted to be shot. We let him write a letter to his family. It wasn't easy killing him, in such a situation. But we couldn't keep them prisoners; we had nowhere to put them. The Maquis leaders decided between them to kill him. Personally, I think, whether he was for Hitler or not, he was a human being. After all he was fighting in a war.

Paul Guerbois, former assistant commander of the FFI in Valençay, was more closely involved with the execution, and he related the details later. A war council was held at Belle Etoile farm in Valençay [Perdriset's headquarters] and the council decided to avenge comrades who had just been killed in atrocious conditions. Pedriset gave the execution order to Paul Guerbois. He assembled a firing squad and read the sentence to the captain, who was sitting in front of an oak tree: he couldn't move because he was hit in both legs.

In the end, however, the captain was shot by one man. There was a deserter from the German army, who was in a Maquis but not with us, still in German army uniform. He was part of the first battalion of Vannier's company. He told Paul Guerbois that he was from Alsace. Just as he was telling Paul this, a dozen German prisoners on their way to fatigue duty passed by, accompanied by the Maquis. The captain called over to them and got them to stand to attention [see note on page 168]. They all saluted, and he suddenly started haranguing them—but not for long because the Alsatian shot him twice in the head with his P38.

Personally I think that someone who hasn't lived through this type of war can't understand what it was really like; it's impossible. Even London had no idea. On September 10, 1944, a column of 18,000 Germans who had been trying to return to Germany [see note on page 169] surrendered to one man, an American from the US Army, in the town of Issoudun. At the time the American press thrived on the story, but they didn't tell the full story. They forgot to mention the column had been harassed by all the Maquis in the sector. The 18,000 German soldiers didn't surrender as easily as that, for no reason, to one American! In addition, the Americans authorized the Germans to cross the region all the way to Orleans with their weapons. The resisters were furious. Always the same old story: armies prefer to deal with armies, and the Resistance wasn't an army.

Major Clutton, with someone from Châteauroux, negotiated the surrender. I wasn't involved. I know that Philippe de Vomécourt was present. But if those 18,000 Germans surrendered in Issoudun, it was because they had been attacked everywhere but refused to surrender to the Maquis. We had to get hold of an American, to whom they surrendered in Orleans. The Allies didn't cross the river Loire so the Germans went to Orleans with their arms.

None of the Maquis was pleased about this. Major Clutton did everything he could to try to stop this business, but it was impossible. Moreover, when the Germans got to the other side of the Loire, the Americans welcomed them with oranges, chocolate, the whole works. But that's an old story, you know, soldiers were welcoming other soldiers. We weren't soldiers.

But at the end of the day, the Americans who were offering oranges probably hadn't fought much against the Germans, not at all. They couldn't understand what had happened.

[After the liberation], in September 1944, when we were still eating at the Maquis staff mess at the Lion d'Or hotel in Valençay, a mission of the Gaullist regional military delegation [representing General Charles de Gaulle—see note on page 169] invited themselves to lunch with us. They came in and sat down at the table. During the meal one of them started talking to Henri in English, because he was wearing British battle dress.

Henri said, "Don't tire yourself speaking English, I'm French." So the chap then said, "Really! Well as a Frenchman in a foreign uniform, I consider you to be a deserter from the French Army."

When everyone was preparing to leave, Henri, who was at the other end of the U-shaped table, was making desperate signs to me. I was in deep conversation with Francis Perdriset's assistant. When he told me what had happened I was completely flabbergasted. I can't tell you how I felt. As if the world had fallen around me; it was awful.

I took the officer who had threatened Henri into another room and asked him what he meant. All he could see fit to say was, "Do you know Colonel Buckmaster is a Francophobe?"

I was so shocked I could hardly utter a word. I managed to splutter, "So, you believe during the war we wandered around with a notice board saying, 'This is a British network, come and join us'?" People came to us for help, they didn't care whether we were English or French, and we fought the war with them.

It was all just politics.

POSTWAR LIFE

Germany surrendered to the Allies on May 7, 1945. The surrender went into effect the following day, May 8, Victory in Europe or V-E Day. But France was liberated sooner, throughout the summer and fall of 1944. This meant that the Maquis—and the SOE agents who had worked with them—were finished with their work at that time as well. Charles de Gaulle, anxious to not credit the British for their help during the Resistance, gave most British SOE agents just 48 hours to leave France upon his return. But since Pearl was a permanent French resident and Henri a French native, they weren't forced to leave like the other members of the SOE. They left France in the fall of 1944 only in order to report back to the SOE offices in London, at which time they were also finally married. Pearl was asked to join several postwar activities as a representative of the SOE, and she also received several awards.

I was sent to France with a personal allowance of 200,000 francs—before the franc was devalued. The person in charge of SOE's budget in London said, "We'd like you to keep accounts; obviously not for small expenses, but for large ones, yes."

When the Maquis started, we had to find money. London sent us some, but we also requisitioned things and borrowed money—we were able to do this. We explained to people that if they wanted a guarantee, the BBC would send a message. They just had to give us their own message and we would instruct the BBC to broadcast it in the evening. This was how they knew London would reimburse them.

I'd been asked to keep accounts, and, being disciplined, I realized it was going to involve fairly large sums of money so thought I'd better do the job properly. Luckily we had Gaëtan Ravineau in our Maquis, and later he became chief treasurer and paymaster. He was still a student at the time, but he knew a good deal about accounting. I asked him if he would take care of the accounts and he did them for all four Maquis until the end. He really put his heart into it because it wasn't an easy job.

When I returned to London in September 1944, I handed over my accounts to the SOE officer, who asked, "What are these?"

"They're accounts of money spent for the Maquis."

"Well it's the first time I've seen anything of the sort."

Nobody ever spoke about these papers detailing my finances with the SOE. I thought they must have got lost and there was no trace of them. Then one day at a dinner of former SOE agents held in Paris in 1994, SOE's archivist at the Foreign Office said, "You know there's a very thick file about you at the office."

"Really?"

"I even saw a paper I thought was strange; it was full of very detailed accounts."

"You're joking, you really have those accounts?"

I could have hugged him. I thought, So they still exist and I'm going to ask for them; I can do that.

Between the four Maquis groups, we ended up spending, if I remember correctly, almost six million francs. The money was used to pay people and to pay for food and other expenses. When we could, we also bought uniforms.

Towards the end of the war we gave money to all the members; I can't remember how much, somewhere between 5 and 20 francs each.

When we arrived in England, Henri had the remaining cash in a suitcase and at the office in London they couldn't believe it. We returned all the remaining money, every last penny.

When I arrived back in London, I was wearing a strange "uniform." Instead of sending me a proper uniform, they had sent me an army khaki battle dress jacket with trousers that were too short and a cap that was too small. I pinched a beret from one of the lads because I had to put something on my head. Philippe de Vomécourt gave me my shoes. They had belonged to Murielle Byck, who was parachuted in as a radio operator and who died of meningitis in Romorantin in the Loir-et-Cher. They were really ski boots, but I didn't have any other shoes to wear. I also had a civilian raincoat, but I'd lost its belt.

Well, that's how I was dressed when I arrived in London. I asked where my uniform was because I wanted to dress correctly. I was told I had to wait; it was in a stock room or something. I waited for a week.

But during the week I wasn't going to remain shut up inside. I went to Regent Street with my sisters and some French people, and we were just about to enter a chemist's [drugstore] when at the last minute I decided to stay outside. Three women were coming out of the shop—I was in the doorway—when I heard one say, "Did you see that funny uniform?" It wasn't a uniform at all. That's how I'm dressed in the photograph with Francis Perdriset, Robert Knéper, and Jim Menzies.

At the time, V2s [German rockets sent from Holland] were exploding all over England. I never saw the V1s in England. They must have been horrifying, because you could hear them but you couldn't see where they were going to explode, whereas the V2s fell silently and exploded afterwards. With a V2 you didn't have time to get worried, you knew it wasn't for you.

Henri and I couldn't marry during the clandestine period because Henri would have been a bigamist. I had forged papers, and he would have married Mademoiselle Vergès instead of Mademoiselle Witherington; it's not the same thing. When we arrived in England, we decided to get married. Naturally we had to wait for the banns to be published [a public announcement required two weeks prior to a British wedding] amongst other formalities.

We were married at a register office in London, on the 26th of October, 1944. My mother and two of my sisters came, plus two or three friends. My third sister, who was married, didn't come. It was the simplest of ceremonies. Henri's family wasn't there because there was no traveling between France and England at the time, except of course for people who were on military missions. So we thought we would have a church wedding in France. But we stayed in England until December.

Then we returned to France on the "Judex Mission": There was Colonel Buckmaster with an assistant, Nancy Fraser-Campbell; a Frenchman representing de Gaulle; Henri and I; Jacqueline Nearne, who was Maurice Southgate's other courier; and, finally, Jones, Philippe de Vomécourt's radio operator. We were to visit the families who had personally helped us SOE agents. We couldn't give them decorations because there weren't any, but the colonel handed out a letter thanking them for the assistance they had given the resistance.

Our first visit was to Doulçay farm to visit the Trochet family. In December 1944 we arrived at the Trochet farm without warning; there were about 10 of us. They weren't expecting us at all. But Grandma Trochet, who was a very good cook, prepared an excellent lunch for 10 people within an hour.

There was also some financial assistance for people who needed it, for example the Sabassier family. We gave them about 20,000 francs. They had lost everything in the fire, absolutely everything; they didn't have a stick of furniture left. The money we gave them helped them to get back to normal.

We also went to Châteauroux, where all our chaps from the Maquis were in barracks. I was welcomed like a queen: "Oh, here's Pauline!" as if I had come from the moon! It was very amusing. I was dressed in RAF uniform. We went to Clermont-Ferrand, then on to Montluçon. A hotel where we stayed during the clandestine period was apparently used by the Gestapo. The Resistance had blown it up. There were no rooms left in the other hotel, so the whole Judex Mission had to sleep in sleeping bags on the floor of a bistro.

We returned to Paris, we were discharged, then we worked on all the papers for a church wedding at L'Oratoire du Louvre [a chapel in Paris] for January 3, 1945. There was hardly anybody at the church wedding: Henri's father, his aunt, his mother, and another witness who was Henri's father's partner. There were six of us—we had the church to ourselves. We were so broke we were married in uniform; we didn't even have our photo taken, honestly. We don't have many souvenirs from our wedding: while we were walking home from the church along the rue du Faubourg Saint-Honoré, we went into a leather goods shop and bought a manicure set. We still have it. And we did prepare a card: "Mrs. Gertrude Witherington has the honour of announcing the marriage of her daughter . . ." We sent that announcement afterward. But, you know, we've never managed to do things like everyone else.

In January 1945, I was summoned to SOE's postwar office in Paris, and the officer there said, "Read this." It was an account of events during part of my mission. I didn't know what it was leading up to until the very end of the text, when I realized that I had been nominated for an MBE [Member of the Most Excellent Order of the British Empire]. But there are two categories of MBE, military and civil. I was on the civil list. I thought, They have a nerve, treating me as though I had spent the war sitting behind a desk. You see, I had been sent to France as a civilian in uniform, therefore I wasn't entitled to a military decoration, something of which I was totally unaware.

I asked the officer, "What's all this about then?"

"It's a press release."

"A what? A civilian decoration? I don't agree with that at all."

"Neither do I," he replied, "get a typewriter and send a reply immediately."

I know it's not the done thing, but I wrote to say I was sorry, a civil decoration wasn't fair. It was the first time they'd sent women to work in an occupied country, and if all they could do was to give me a civil decoration then I didn't want it. Either they did things properly or not at all. I said that I hadn't done anything remotely civil for England during the war.

It stirred up such a fuss, what a reaction. Even the French press covered the story. I had no idea it would create such a stir.

Later, in February 1946, I received a phone call from Vera Atkins in London. She said, "You've been asked to go to America." I was to participate in a series of conferences on England's role in the war. And who should I bump into there? My former boss, Douglas Colyer, who was then head of the RAF delegation in the United States. He saw me arrive in uniform with all the French decorations. I wasn't wearing the MBE.

He said, in a tone he'd never used before, "What's all this business about the MBE?" I told him my side of the story, and he replied, "Well, whatever happened, you cannot tour America wearing all those French decorations and not the English one. Put it on, it's an order."

I said, "All right, but as soon as I leave America I'm taking it off, because I don't want it."

The speaker who preceded me on the American tour's roster was Constance Babington-Smith, the WAAF who located Peenemünde research station for V1s and V2s on the Baltic coast, by examining aerial photos taken by the RAF. Douglas Colyer must have thought that it would also be a good idea to send a WAAF who had been in field work. The tour included New York, Washington, Cleveland, Chicago, Detroit, Buffalo, and Philadelphia. The conferences were held in schools, clubs, and so on, of which there are many in the US, and I spoke about the role of the Resistance and the SOE.

In one city there was a large German American community, but nobody had warned me. Whilst I was talking I could feel there was some discomfort. After the talk, an American approached me and he said, "Do you think all Germans are like that?"

To get out of it I said, "I don't know, I only saw Nazis!"

On the way back to England, I was on the same liner—the *Queen Mary*—as Douglas Colyer. As I was an honorary flight officer and wanted to speak to him—an air marshal—I had to go through his aide-de-camp to arrange a meeting.

I went to his cabin and said, "Now we're alone, let me explain why I refused the MBE." I told him everything and asked him if he thought it was fair. I reminded him that when he was in Paris he always grumbled that the Administration, with a capital A, never understood anything. These decorations were governed by certain rules, but now the rules had to be changed. The type of mission carried out by all the women sent to France was unprecedented in British war history.

He didn't make any comment at the time, but in September 1946 I was finally awarded the military MBE along with several other SOE women agents and one man, a former radio operator. I received the MBE from the British ambassador but not in the embassy itself. The ceremony was in a building on the corner of the rue d'Aguesseau that belonged to the Roger Gallet firm. General De Larminat was present, and when my nomination was announced, he applauded—which was unheard of.

I parachuted four times: three in training—two day jumps and one at night—and the fourth was in operation, when I landed in France. The SOE men all jumped four times in training and a fifth in operation, which gave them the right to wear wings, the parachutists' license for which you needed five jumps. When I got back to England after the war I was told, "No, you can't wear wings, you have only jumped four times."

This was their way of granting the award to men only. I didn't care. I had jumped, I went into operation; I was going to wear them [see note on page 169].

From December 1944 until April 1948, apart from the two-to-three-month mission in the States, I was "without a profession"; in other words, I took care of my husband and our home in Rue de Buci. When our daughter, Claire, was born on April 7, 1948, I took her to Doulçay farm.

Immediately after the war, life in Paris was very difficult, especially when compared with modern life. There weren't all the facilities there are today such as washing machines, disposable nappies [diapers], telephones, televisions, taxis, cars, and so forth. People today can't imagine how we lived: there was no coffee, no tea, no cocoa, no milk except for children under 14, no potatoes. Sugar and bread were rationed; we had 50 grams [less than two ounces, about a third of a stick] of butter a week and 350 grams [about three-quarters of a pound] of meat, plus three hours queuing to get it!

Gas pressure was so low that we blocked every other hole in the burner with bread crumbs. We had 200 kilos of coal for the whole winter [about one-tenth of the normal requirement]. I used to light the fire just before Henri came home from work. It was only 3°C [37°F] in the bedroom. We had to make do with what we had.

When Henri came to the farm from Paris [in August 1948], our daughter was four months old. He said, "We've lost everything; the business has gone bust [see note on page 170]." He hadn't even had enough money to take the train; he had to come back to Doulçay from Paris by bike! We were absolutely penniless.

I asked him, "What are we going to do?"

When he replied, "I don't know," I was panic stricken. We owe so much to the French because the Trochet family looked after Henri and our daughter at the farm while I returned to Paris. It was easier for me to find a job.

Someone had maliciously spread a rumor that we had received gold and platinum ingots [bars of pure precious metals] by parachute, but it wasn't true. And no one was ever capable of saying what we'd bought with them! When the Trochets bought Jaugy, a château in Gièvres in the Loir-et-Cher *departement*, they were accused of using them: "With all the ingots you received during the war you could afford it." No ingots were ever parachuted, none, of any kind!

When I arrived in Paris from the farm I was lucky. My former boss, Air Marshal Douglas Colyer, whom I liked very much, had been transferred to the embassy in Paris just after the war. So I went to see him, told him about our problems, and explained that I absolutely had to find a job. He said, "All right, I'll see to it." He gave me three to choose from. That's how I started working in the Canadian embassy in August 1948. None of this work was linked to my work during the war and the Resistance. We just needed to cope, to find work. We had to start all over again.

After seven years at the Canadian embassy, I worked at the World Bank for a total of 28 years. For the first seven years there I had a boss who wanted me to be available 24 hours a day. On three occasions when I was given a salary raise, he said, "You'd better organize your life so you can give all your time to the World Bank." I had a hard time, but I put up with it because I had no choice. I cried all weekend. Then I worked for John Miller at the World Bank for 12 years. They were the happiest because we worked like clockwork together.

In the end I was given the job of librarian, which quickly turned to research assistant. I was in charge of sending out all the documentation on the organizations that were part of the World Bank and on the Bank itself. I sent literature to Europe, Africa, and even Indochina. I was quite busy.

RIGHTING WRONGS

Although the SOE was officially disbanded on January, 15, 1946, on orders from the new prime minister, Clement Attlee (and its personnel files sealed until 2004), there were still many mysteries left to unravel. For instance, Vera Atkins received authorization, paid for by the SIS (MI6), to travel to Germany in order to uncover the fate of the 52 SOE agents (12 of them women) who had failed to return.

One of the biggest mysteries surrounding the SOE involved H. A. E. Déricourt, an SOE agent involved with SOE's Prosper network in Paris, who was highly suspected of being a double agent. When one of Pearl's friends was arrested, most likely because of Déricourt, Pearl was determined to help him.

She also took action in a matter of recognition for those who had risked their lives for France. After the war, many members of the French Resistance were highly decorated by the de Gaulle government. However, those French resisters who had worked with the SOE were often slighted due to de Gaulle's attitude toward the British. This greatly offended Pearl's sense of justice.

Just after the war we spent many evenings with Armel Guerne and his wife, Périgrine. He was a writer and poet. You could discuss anything with him; I could listen to him for hours. Sometimes we talked until three in the morning! He and his wife enriched our lives a great deal. Armel had worked very hard in France supporting the Prosper SOE network. He was intent on fighting the Germans. That's why he didn't understand why the English imprisoned him on his arrival there after the liberation.

When he first arrived he was interrogated by the Intelligence Service—as were all the people who arrived during the war—but he didn't tell them everything. That's how I see it. He must have kept silent about the Germans having microfilms of correspondence between the networks and England. Maybe they sensed he was withholding information. So they put him in prison. Putting someone in prison because he was suspected of not telling everything wasn't usually done in Britain. You weren't locked up when you didn't tell everything; you were kept and interrogated, but you weren't put behind bars! But Armel was sent to prison and, to cap it all, with Germans. He was in a world apart, and, believe it or not, the prison guard was a German soldier! It's a dreadful story.

We tried hard to help him. First I went to the British embassy in Paris. I rang London to ask if they could give me some information on the way he had been treated. I realized I was knocking my head against a brick wall. Some time after this, the British embassy told me there was an organization that took care of all the SOE networks in France. I went to see them. I met the famous Dr. Balachowski and a certain Monsieur Durand, who was the president of the free resistance federation Fédération Nationale Libre Résistance, also called Amicale Buckmaster.

I said, "I would like to know why Monsieur Guerne has so many problems." All the members of the Prosper network were in the same boat; they didn't understand why they had been arrested. They had been trapped in the most horrible net. On top of that, Armel Guerne found himself confronting the French police, who also accused him of being a traitor. He thought he was going to end up in prison a second time—he had already been arrested by the Gestapo in 1943 and had escaped from Buchenwald—which was something he could not stomach!

I asked these men for help because I thought that was their responsibility. But I learned they passed directly to the police any statements from people accusing Armel Guerne of treachery.

"What?" I said, "You're supposed to be an organization helping people who fought in the Resistance, and you send these statements directly to the police, without giving Armel Guerne the possibility of defending himself? What's that supposed to mean?" Do you know what they replied? "Madame, we only have one piece of advice to give you: keep out of this matter."

I said, "Messieurs, when I undertake something, I keep at it until the end and you're not going to stop me!"

I also questioned Vera Atkins, former colleague of Colonel Buckmaster. "I don't know what to say," she replied, "but I'll investigate the matter." After a while she called me. She said, "There's been a gross error." The error was caused by names being confused. That was possible because at the time we didn't know H. A. E. Déricourt was behind the whole affair. I said to Vera Atkins, "As Colonel Buckmaster is kind enough to visit me each time he comes to Paris, can you ask him to alert me next time. I'll ask Armel Guerne to come too." I added, "For Armel it will be enough knowing, for his own self-respect and peace of mind, that it was a mistake. Even if it's just verbal." The colonel never came to see me again at home.

The matter was never completely cleared up. It's all part of the mystery—the Prosper mystery. And there were other victims, and I'll explain why. Because when Prosper and the others were in the "sorting centre" in Compiègne—the last step before being deported—they tried to understand why they had all been trapped. Jacques Bureau and Prosper [Francis Suttill], Gilbert Norman, and all the members of the network tried to understand why they had been caught in the net, and why the Gestapo had microfilms of documents sent to London from France. They concluded, "Someone in England has betrayed us." In fact, it was Déricourt who was handing over these documents to the Germans. He handled a lot of correspondence because he was in charge of the landings and takeoffs of the Lysander planes, which transported agents, leaders, messages, and so on.

In France, people finally realized that something was not quite right with Déricourt's work. When they went to England they told the SOE office, but the English wouldn't believe it; they were pleased with Déricourt's results. Only one person said she didn't agree, because she didn't trust Déricourt: Vera Atkins.

Following these complaints and suspicions from France, the office finally called Déricourt back to London. But he was put under surveillance in a hotel, not in prison. He wasn't sent back to France again. He wasn't cleared then: he hadn't been tried; that came much later. He returned to France in 1945, was tried by court marshal, and [Nicholas] Bodington, a former SOE staff member, testified in his favor and he was cleared. I don't know how he managed it.

Déricourt had a German card and agent number. Professor Michael Foot, the SOE historian, found that out when he was questioning a Gestapo agent in Germany who had worked with Déricourt. Michael Foot stated that in Déricourt's opinion, only one person mattered, or rather two: himself and his wife. Later Déricourt went to Indochina. He appeared in court a second time accused of gold and currency trafficking. He was let off and switched to drugs trafficking. All in all he was an undesirable character! In the end he was killed in a private plane crash.

Armel Guerne died a long time after the war. He bought a mill somewhere in the Lot department; he passed away there. But he wrote an account of his life that was published in Australia, in English, which meant no one could read it in France. Much later it was translated into French and photocopied. The good thing about this story is that we were the ones who insisted he should write it. "With all those stories you have to tell, you should write a book. You must write your memoirs." We really badgered him into it.

Philippe de Vomécourt, who was president of the Fédération Nationale Libre Résistance after the liberation, said to me one day, "The final list of nominations for the Legion of Honour for resistance fighters is coming up. You'll see, we'll be left out again. We'll be ignored; it's as good as done!"

Later at work, I was reading the *Journal Officiel* when I noticed that Livry-Level, whom I had met at my second parachute attempt, was on the Legion of Honor committee. I thought I might be able to see him. He was in the same situation as we were: as a former RAF pilot he was scorned by the French services, and he had had trouble with "La France Libre," the French who were with de Gaulle in London.

First I asked de Vomécourt how many resisters deserved to be decorated. There were 42. I asked for an appointment with Livry-Level.

When I saw him, I said, "I don't know if you remember me, we met . . ."

"Of course, I remember perfectly."

"I've come to ask you a favor. You can't have forgotten all the trouble you've had because you were in the RAF. Well I'm so disgusted with all the problems the French who worked with the British networks are having. I'd like to ask you for help for the next list of nominations for the Legion of Honor."

"How many cases are there?"

"There are 42."

"OK, let me have the files."

Philippe de Vomécourt then organized a meeting with Livry-Level, and the 42 were nominated. But I swear if I hadn't done that, not one would have received it. Once more it was a matter of luck; simply because I could read the *Journal Officiel* and I was fairly sure Livry-Level would help us.

Henri was one of the 42; so was Jean-Bernard Badaire, who became president of the Fédération Nationale Libre Résistance in 1983. Philippe de Vomécourt decorated them with the Legion of Honor in a private ceremony at the club of the Free French Forces!

But the French who had worked with the SOE continued to be slighted by the French government. A small example is Jean-Bernard Badaire, who returned to Saint-Cyr military school after the war, and who had worked with the SOE, learned that his military record contained the statement, "May have worked for a foreign allied power." A foreign allied power!

Finally, in 1993, I asked to speak during the annual meeting of the National Confederation of the French Fighting Forces that was composed of three French federations. I asked for an explanation. I said that after 50 years we were fed up with this unconstructive treatment. I am really appalled and annoyed to see how the French Resistance members of the British networks are considered as nonentities. After all, I pulled quite a few French people into mine.

Heavens, during the war, I didn't care whether I was working with the French or the English. For me it was the same thing. Politics are all very well, but when you want to get rid of an enemy, I'm afraid, as far as I'm concerned, politics have nothing to do with it. I never mixed in politics, and I never will.

CONCLUSION

Nothing is completed easily in life, and this book took a lot of time and dedication from both Henri and me. We wanted to tell our story as it happened and as we experienced it.

I hope this testimony will help young people get over the problems and difficulties that happen in any life. Never lose hope, never give in, because life will not make things easy, but it knows how to reward those who approach it conscientiously, bravely, and with determination.

We have both come to the end of our lives by facing life together and by creating a close circle of friends who were chosen for their humanity. We would like to thank them with all our hearts for being so wonderful.

—PEARL WITHERINGTON CORNIOLEY
AND HENRI CORNIOLEY, 1995

EPILOGUE

Whatever Pauline asked us to do, we accepted quite voluntarily. We obeyed her. She was for us what de Gaulle was for France. She had become our symbol. For myself, I held her in great admiration. She has a sensibility for being "in company" with men, a sense of friendship, which not all women have—though she is an advocate for women.

At the first reunion of the Amicale North-Indre Cher Valley, there were more than 300. Pauline was there. You should have seen the rush toward Pauline—it was unbelievable! Of the 300, there were about 20, even still, who knew her personally. As Louis Belliard says, "Everyone knows Madame Pauline, but no one has ever seen her." She had become "our national Pauline"! A foreigner, and a woman, who had fallen from the sky—all this surpasses the imagination. We did not think that a woman could do that, especially at that time. And then, she was pretty. It was she who arranged the parachute drops, she who was our idol; it was through our connection with her that we fought.

—RAYMOND BILLARD, "GASPARD," ONE OF
PEARL'S LIEUTENANTS AND A FORMER
MEMBER OF THE WRESTLER CIRCUIT

Pearl passed away February, 24, 2008, at a hospital in Blois, France, in her 94th year, after having lived a decade at a retirement home in Chateauvieux. At that home she proved true to her nature, encouraging the other residents with consideration and patience, busying herself with internal proceedings, and extending her independence as long as possible. Hervé Larroque kept in touch with her during this time and, describing their last telephone conversation, he said that Pearl "was keen to listen and ready to laugh if the occasion called for it. It is the strength and the courage in that laugh that remains my last memory of this great lady."

ACKNOWLEDGMENTS

I'm grateful to M. Hervé Larroque for entrusting to me with the task of shaping the precious material he garnered from his personal interviews with Pearl Witherington Cornioley. I'd also like to thank him and my husband, John, for their innumerable interlanguage communications in which they precisely hammered out translation renderings, geography, and photograph identification. John, your tireless attention to detail was especially appreciated during your review of the original French against the English translation, which proved to be an illuminating and clarifying effort.

I'd like to thank my editor, Lisa Reardon, for her insightful insistence that I place the material within a framework suitable for young adult readers and for making many other helpful suggestions along the way.

Thanks also to Michelle Schoob for cheerfully fielding some last-minute changes and to Chris Erichsen for his beautiful work on the maps.

The attempt to make an accurate map from Pearl Witherington's understated description of her difficult travels out of occupied France begged the addition of some detail, so a special note of thanks is due to two people for their help in this regard: M. Pierre Vergnon, a current resident of Genélard (Saône et Loire), France, near where Pearl very likely crossed the line of demarcation, and who was a nine-year-old boy at the time; and Sébastien Joly, a historian specializing in the demarcation line, professor of history and geography (Saône-et-Loire). Their insights helped to form a clear picture of what it must have been like for four women fleeing the Nazis to get off a train in rural France in December 1940 and make their way cross-country to Vichy, more than 68 miles away, without a vehicle.

And finally, special thanks to Sarah Olson for her impressive book jacket design; I wouldn't have thought it possible to come so close to a visual distillation of Pearl Witherington's SOE career, but apparently I was wrong.

KEY FIGURES

Vera Atkins

Officially the French (F) Section's intelligence officer and Maurice Buckmaster's personal assistant, some considered Vera Atkins to be the real power in the F Section. She acted as a liaison between headquarters and the agents' families (Pearl Witherington's mother received a handwritten note from Atkins in response to each of her numerous enquiries regarding Pearl's welfare). Atkins took a trip to Germany after the war to personally discover the fate of the F Section agents who didn't return.

Raymond Billard ("Gaspard")

A discharged French sailor who became one of Pearl's lieutenants in the Marie-Wrestler network, Billard was one of the first resisters to encounter the Germans during the Battle of Les Souches. He is currently the secretary of Editions par exemple, the publishers of Pearl Witherington's French memoir.

"Alex" Briant

The FTP leader in the North Indre network, Alex Briant served as a deputy under the leadership of the Gaullist Armond Mardon, the mayor of Dun-le-Poelier until his arrest in June 1944. He worked with Pearl Witherington after she assumed leadership of the area.

Maurice Buckmaster

Often referred to as "the Colonel," Maurice Buckmaster had been an army intelligence officer before being made the head of the SOE's F Section.

Auguste Chantraine ("Octave")

A farmer in the town of Tendu, near Chateauroux, and the mayor, he was an early leader in the Resistance in Indre. He became a key figure in the northern part of Maurice Southgate's Stationer network, successfully pulling together several small FTP groups in the area willing to work with the SOE. Many drops of personnel (including Pearl Withergton) and supplies took place on his farm. He was arrested by the Germans and later executed at Mauthausen concentration camp in the spring of 1945.

Douglas Colyer

Pearl Witherington's boss at the British embassy prior to the war who helped her find employment after the war.

Emile Coulaudon ("Gaspard")

A leader in the Auvergne Resistance and the director of their sabotage efforts. After the leaders of the SOE's Headmaster network were arrested, the Auvergne group was given assistance from Maurice Southgate in the Stationer network.

Charles de Gaulle
One of the only French military leaders who led his men to victory during the Battle of France, de Gaulle fled to London after being condemned to death in absentia for vocally opposing the surrender to Germany. There he became an inspiring leader—broadcasting radio messages and training servicemen—to many French people who wanted to resist the collaboration with Germany, but his relationship with British leaders during the war was always strained.

Jacques Hirsch
A French resister who worked extensively with the Stationer network and whose entire family was involved in the Resistance.

Henri Ingrand
A medical doctor who was involved in various Resistance activities from the beginning of the occupation, he was a cofounder in 1943 of the Auvergne resistance, where he remained to the end of the war.

Philippe Livry-Level
A French airman during World War I, Livry-Level escaped Nazi-occupied France and joined the RAF, lying about his age (he was too old), flying many successful missions, and receiving numerous awards.

Amédée Maingard
Initially trained to be a radio operator for the Stationer network, Amédée Maingard also became Maurice Southgate's assistant organizer and later helped Pearl organize the huge network into sections, eventually taking control of the Shipwright network himself.

Armand Mardon

The mayor of Dun-le-Poelier, the town near the Battle of Les Souches, and a Gaullist resistance leader of the North Indre resistance before Pearl took it over. He was found out and arrested by the Gestapo on June 1, 1944, shortly after the arrest and questioning of Maurice Southgate.

Jacqueline Nearne

Born in Britain to an English father and French mother, Jacqueline was raised in France but escaped to England when France was invaded by Germany. Because she was fluent in French, she was recruited by SOE's F Section and became a courier for the Stationer network (but her path rarely crossed with Pearl's).

Francis Perdriset

A French army captain from Châteauroux (the secret headquarters of the AS and the FFI in the Indre area), who responded to Pearl's request for a military commander. He worked with the Maquis of the Marie-Wrestler network.

Marshall Pétain

A beloved French hero of World War I, Marshall Pétain became the leader of Vichy France, the collaborationist French government during World War II, and as such he—and his army of military police, the Milice—became enemies to the French Resistance.

Gaëtan Ravineau

A Maquis from the Marie-Wrestler network who functioned as its chief treasurer and paymaster. He is currently the vice president of Editions par exemple, the publisher of Pearl Witherington's French memoir.

The Sabassier family
This family lived in the guardhouse of the Les Souches estate and provided shelter to those in the disrupted Stationer network for a month prior to D-day. The Sabbasiers were directly involved in the Battle of Les Souches.

Maurice Southgate ("Hector Stationer")
The very capable leader/organizer of the F Section's enormous Stationer network, Maurice Southgate was an old schoolmate of Pearl Witherington's, and she specifically requested to join his network. After his arrest, Pearl helped divide the Stationer network into four separate networks.

The Trochet family
Pearl and Henri found refuge on the farm of this rural French family immediately after Maurice Southgate's arrest. Pearl affectionately referred to the mother and father as Grandpa and Grandma Trochet.

Philippe de Vomécourt ("Saint Paul")
A French resister who allowed the very first F Section weapons drop to occur on his land, de Vomécourt—who had lost his father in World War I and whose two brothers were SOE agents—became heavily involved in Resistance activities, was trained briefly by the SOE at one point, and escaped from capture several times (being once imprisoned at the Prison of Saint Paul, hence his code name).

APPENDIX

EXTRACTS FROM ORIGINAL INTERVIEWS

Henri's Story

Henri, what about your social and family origins?

Henri: My family ran a beauty salon, which was in a huge apartment on the rue du Faubourg Saint-Honoré. I had an extraordinary golden childhood. I had to sweat it out later in life but it didn't bother me. The beauty business was extremely profitable; we lived in the lap of luxury.

I left school when I was 16. From 1926 to 1930—the year I left for my military service in Tunisia—I worked for my father's company and learned how to make cosmetics and perfumes. During the day I worked in the laboratory; in the evening I was a delivery boy. But when I returned from Tunisia I was employed with my brother in a factory that manufactured building site lamps and fire extinguishers. In 1938, I started a small business with a friend making liquid carpet-cleaning products.

We were called up for military service in 1939, and I did the same as everyone else; in other words, not a lot. We were waiting for "them" to arrive. I was sent to a place near Sedan, where I played cards, usually *belote* [a popular French card game similar to bridge], throughout the winter. I was given leave in February 1940, then following the German attack of May 10, my regiment went north almost as far as Belgium—I can't say if we reached Belgium or not. At least we made the effort to go that far! The Germans gave us a thrashing, so we turned round and headed south. I was imprisoned just south of Verdun.

The first winter in the Ardennes, from 1939 to 1940, wasn't exactly a piece of cake. I was in the 19th horse regiment. We spent most of our time burying horses that were dropping like flies. To bury a horse you need to dig a big hole, and the ground was frozen solid. Luckily I didn't have to dig. I had a privileged position; I was a machine-gunner. Can you imagine that, machine guns against airplanes, it's not exactly good anti-aircraft defense—efficiency-wise it was bordering on useless! But we never made any mistakes during that war. Every time we saw a plane, we fired. We were sure they were all German, because the French didn't have any *(laughing)*!

Did you often hit them?

German planes would occasionally fly over, but we were never really attacked. We'd set up the machine gun in a field because we had been told always to go behind the hedgerows to keep out of view. When planes flew over—ratatata . . . fearless we were! We fired away until one day the lieutenant shouted at us, "You just don't realize, you're firing like that, but do you have any idea how much each bullet costs?"

"No idea," I replied.

"Each one costs a franc!"

"Well, each round is pretty expensive then, but after all, we are here to fire."

We were firing too many rounds and each bullet cost a franc.

Really (laughing)!

I'm not joking, it's the truth. Then we were surprised we lost the war *(laughing)*.

I have other beauties like that to tell.

It was freezing cold even though we were slightly protected with our uniforms and the rest of our kit. We were in a village called Beaumont-en-Argonne near Vouziers, in the Ardennes. It's pretty nippy up there in winter and there was snow.

We knew everyone in Beaumont-en-Argonne. They treated us royally. We often went to the mayor's, who was very kind to us. He kept rabbit hutches, with little rabbits, so you can imagine. Little rabbits are so sweet, all baby animals are. One of his rabbits had a litter of five or six bunnies and one of them, just one, was completely black. I don't know who she'd been with!

When the Germans attacked, we went up to Belgium, then about a week later we were stopped by the German advance, so we did an about-turn. We retreated the way we had come and got back to the same village where we were forced to spend a night.

There was not a living soul; everyone had evacuated and the village had been completely pillaged. It must have been French soldiers who had done that because the Germans were behind us and hadn't gotten that far. I've never seen anything like it, it was dreadful.

I went to the mayor's house and noticed that the hutches had been opened. All the little rabbits were running about in the wild. The rabbits that could be eaten had been pinched [stolen], but there were loads that had been killed for the sake of killing. Then I remembered my black rabbit. I decided to try to find it. There were rabbits everywhere. After a while I managed to put my hands on it and said, "Listen mate, you're coming with me."

We left the next day and I took my rabbit with me. He was quite small. We continued retreating to Verdun and I still had my rabbit. He was completely spoilt because we were in a horse regiment and had as much oat as we needed for the horses. You can imagine how he stuffed himself. There was no shortage of grass either.

We were in the machine gun section, therefore every time we stationed somewhere we had to take up positions outside the station area, in a field or on a hill—supposedly to attack German planes. I'd take the rabbit every time. He was completely tame. He never tried to escape. He would stay with me even when we were firing the machine gun. He was used to it. He was really cute, my little rabbit.

The other lads in the section teased me. Every time we had to move on, they'd say, "Hey Cornioley, don't forget the rabbit." We got to the south of Verdun, where we were dismissed. We knew we were going to be taken prisoners when the Germans arrived in the space of an afternoon. We didn't keep anything. We even heated some coffee by burning bank notes. I picked up my rabbit and said, "Listen you, my time's up but you're a rabbit, you can escape. Now hop along." And since that day there have been black rabbits in Lorraine.

It's the only life I saved during the war!

The winter passed and the debacle came. We did the same as nearly everybody else: a lot of running away. It didn't warm us up very much, but it was a good time of the year. Then came the first winter in Germany, oh–la-la. It wasn't nearly as comfortable and the food was worse. It wasn't half cold; it was freezing, awful. The next war I fight will be in Africa; at any rate, it won't be in a country where it's so cold in winter. You know it's one of the main reasons I escaped from Germany.

(laughing)

I'm not joking!

That winter I said to myself, Well mate, you're not spending another winter here. I don't know what's going to happen,
but you'll not stay here. And that's just what happened when
circumstances made it easy for me—or rather for us, there were
five of us who escaped from there.

Did you know someone who could get you the right papers?

Not at all, we left without any papers. We were in a camp, in
fact we built the camp. We built absolutely everything, even the
barbed-wire fencing. In some places we put up so much fencing
that prisoners escaped by throwing two blankets over it. They
got across as easy as pie. We reckoned that if we used enough
barbed wire when escaping prisoners climbed over, it wouldn't
collapse.

After that, for a while a "commando of barbs" was formed.
We were on the Siegfried line and our job was to take down all
the barbed wiring along the line. Maybe it was sent to Russia; in
any case, it disappeared.

When the spring came, we became a "farming commando":
that was the second phase. We harvested crops. What a com-
edy! All the lads wanted to stack the sheaves on the cart, but
the stacking isn't that straightforward. As long as the cart's not
moving, it's easy, but as soon as it sets off, if they aren't well
balanced—crash, bang, wallop! It's driven three yards, they all
tumble down and you have to start all over again.

Another funny thing happened to me. There was a little
wood near the camp. After working for a while, I thought I'd
had enough—we were allowed to stop briefly when nature
called. So I left the others, found myself a nice little spot, and

thought I might as well have a snooze. At that time I could sleep anyhow and anywhere. I fell fast asleep.

When I woke up, all the others had gone back to the camp. They hadn't noticed I was missing because no one counted the prisoners outside; we were only counted when we got back to camp. I wondered what I was going to do; I hadn't prepared anything for an escape, was wearing clogs and so on. So, I decided I'd better go back to the camp and explain.

I arrived at the camp, asked for an interpreter, told him what had happened, and asked him to get me in. He went to tell the camp commander and came back five minutes later: "You can't come in. They don't want you to enter; they've had a head count and it was correct *(laughing)*."

I said, "But, this just isn't on, I have to enter." They discussed it for a while, obviously the idiot who had counted didn't want to admit that he'd got it wrong! I said to the interpreter, "It's your word and mine against his; you know me, you know I'm in this camp." What a situation! In the end they let me in.

Sometimes, when we were being counted, we changed places on purpose so they got it wrong and had to start the roll-call again. This meant we started work later.

Pearl: But there are lots of stories about the Germans muddling up their counts. They were hopeless at counting.

Henri: The third phase we were dispersed across the region in small groups to clear up village roads. We collected rubbish, although there wasn't much of it; people only chucked out real waste. Everything else was used. There must have been about 30 of us in the camp. I can't remember if there was a guard, maybe. Each morning we all had our work to do. One day a man asked for four or five men to help him. We went with him and he took us to a nearby canal. The same thing happened, the next day and the next. At lunchtime they brought us thick soup, which was very filling, spot on. In the evening he came to take us back to the camp. To start with, we wondered what we were supposed to be doing there, but until the very end we didn't understand why we were there. It was July, the weather was nice, so we swam and lay in the sun.

During the last days, he didn't even bother to come and fetch us. We made our own way back to the camp. One day I said, "Listen, for the past two weeks we've been well fed and watered, we haven't lifted a finger, we've had a lot of rest. If we want to escape, it's now or never." So with two or three other lads from the camp we decided to leave.

One morning, we headed along the track to the canal and escaped. It wasn't exactly difficult. We followed a road then crossed some fields. We knew that we mustn't be caught by the camp's guards—we'd have been beaten up. But the other Germans, the ones who weren't from the camp, didn't give a damn. If they caught you, they'd just take you to a camp where they rounded up escapees, it wasn't nearly as bad.

We walked for 48 hours, not in any old direction we knew roughly where we were. That's how we escaped.

I was wearing Wellington boots. You can't imagine how much I suffered in them because of the heat. Luckily I had a needle and thread with me. The thread was black so you could see it—and do you know that the best way of popping a blister is to push in the needle and thread it through, then leave the thread so the liquid can run out. When I got to France the soles of my feet had been completely darned.

There was thread everywhere!

Henri: Yes. Not only was it hot when we set off, but there were tremendous thunderstorms. Our feet got wet, our boots filled up, we had to empty them as we went along. At the Donon Pass we were shattered, tired, completely lost, and we walked bang slap into a check point. Three of the four lads who escaped with me were arrested. I managed to escape with the fourth. We went back to the woodman's hut from where we'd started. Next morning, we tried again and as we were crossing the road, a German sentry we hadn't noticed fired warning shots. Instead of stopping we each legged it down different paths towards the plain. I was totally lost; I saw a farmer and asked him where I was. He said, "So, you've escaped then? Do you realize you've just passed a German post? Go to the house over there, they'll help you." It was the mayor's house and I spent the night in his attic. I was in Raon-la-Plaine [Vosges].

The next day someone cycled with me to another village where I took three more escapees under my wing: two Polish men and a North African. None of them could speak any French. I guided them until September 1, 1941, when we arrived in Bourg-en-Bresse and had really escaped. Two days later I was discharged and went to Mâcon to join a "national manpower group" [discharged soldiers].

I didn't leave it until April 1943, when Maurice Southgate managed to send me the following message: "I can give you news about your fiancée whose name is a precious stone." I met Maurice in Tarbes; he told me that Pearl wanted to make sure that I was in France before starting her training to be parachuted. As for the fifth escapee, I only got news from him much later in Marseilles. You should have seen the welcome he gave me, nothing was too much.

Pearl: Before Maurice Southgate left London for France, he asked me to describe in detail the military background of a Frenchman. He needed a cover story for an agent who would use the story if he were captured by the police or the Germans. I gave him the only real-life story I knew, which was that of my fiancé.

When Henri first met Amédée Maingard, Maurice Southgate's radio operator, they started chatting. Henri asked him questions about his military background and Amédée told his story. Henri was so surprised, he kept asking, "Why did we never meet?" because he had been in all the places Amédée gave, which was hardly surprising because it was Henri's military background!

Pearl and Henri's Opinions of the War, the SOE, the Maquis, and the Differences Between the French and the English

Were you always confident, or were there moments when . . .

P: I never had any doubt about the outcome of the war, never. I went to help, persuaded that everything would turn out for the best. I did not know how it would end, I did not know where "they" were going to fall, be beaten. We lived from one day to the next and couldn't do otherwise.

It's strange the questions young people ask. You ask that, but you must realize that everything that was happening to us was so enormous; we just had to find a way through. If we hadn't been convinced that we would succeed, we would never have managed! We were in it up to our necks. We had to say "no, no, no" to the very end.

H: Germany couldn't have won that war because we were sure that one day America would join in, and even if they didn't, they would have given such arms support to the English and the Allies that Germany would have had too many fronts to defend. It was impossible. For starters, the German army was spread over far too wide a territory. Do you realize the extent of their occupation at that time? It was horrifying.

P: Can you try to explain exactly what you want to know?

If Hitler had not attacked the U.S.S.R. can it be sure that he would have been beaten? After all, there have been other enemies who have conquered nations, moved in and remained there—

P: We didn't think about it as deeply as that.

Or, should the situation be compared to someone who has a serious illness and only has one choice; either he considers that he is lost and gives in, or he fights continuously, with all his strength to beat the illness. Maybe in those circumstances you don't weigh up the chances of success. You just say to yourself there is one aim, one objective—

P: That's the answer. You know, when it comes down to it, we couldn't foresee much. Everything was in the hands of the army. Everything went very badly for a long time: in Africa, the situation started changing after General Koenig had done his Bir-Hakeim [an important and successful delaying action staged by the 1st Free French Army against Rommel's Afrika Korps in North Africa]. Then, little by little, things improved. We felt very strongly that "it was going to happen," there was no alternative.

H: As the Germans had not managed to neutralize England, it became a fixed obsession of theirs, an abscess.

P: England was determined—that's for sure. The English, all of them, were in it up to their necks. When I arrived in England in July 1941, I saw Londoners go down into the tube [subway] stations in the evenings to shelter from the bombing. In London the stations are very deep underground. Three tiers of bunk beds had been built along the platforms. People would go down every night with their belongings and rest between the last night train and the morning one.

To come back to your "work" as a courier, by arming the Maquis you were also giving them the means to attack.

P: Maquis were something very new, they hadn't existed before.

H: Don't say they never existed; there were Francs-Tireurs in 1870 who were *maquisards.*

P: Yes but the Francs-Tireurs were soldiers

H: They were still clandestine.

P: We weren't soldiers. Even today, the French Resistance has kept this image: seen from the outside, it was not part of the army, it wasn't part of anything official—except at the end when the Forces Françaises de l'Intérieur came under General Koenig's command.

When you say "from the outside" do you mean from the army's point of view?

P: From the army's point of view or from any other constituted body. We were not a constituted body. We were invented with a single goal in mind, "Set Europe ablaze," as Churchill said, and when the war was over, SOE was disbanded. For a long time SOE was forgotten and ignored—it is still widely unknown in England. You know, SOE was invited to the Festival of Remembrance—a festival where there are representatives from all the British armed forces—for the first time in November 1994. I received an invitation for this commemoration, which takes place every year on November 11 at the Royal Albert Hall in London.

H: In England very few people know the meaning of SOE; it's even less well known than in France.

P: Exactly.

In France people can still remember the radio "Ici Londres" ("This is London"), the parachute drops.

H: Also there are people who lived with SOE agents. For example in the Loir-et-Cher, there were people "in the know"; they knew about SOE.

P: Yes, but why? It's because we formed the Amicale and talked about our work. What I also try to make people understand is that SOE didn't only exist in one region. You know, there were 92 SOE networks in France, formed between 1941 and 1944. The south of the Loire was liberated thanks to these networks; the Allies didn't even need to cross the Loire River.

Which changed the balance of power.

P: After the war Eisenhower and Montgomery said they had saved 15 Allied divisions.

H: Some Maquis in Brittany did a substantial amount of work. I don't mean the big ones, the big ones were disastrous.

P: It was better not to be too big.

H: There were the Maquis of the Vercors, Glières, and Mont-Mouchet.

P: There is a great difference between a member of a Maquis and a soldier. In my opinion, you can't make a *maquisard* out of a soldier.

P: You have to remember that when you had something to do with a service working for the war, you didn't even try to understand it. I never set foot in the office of the section for which I worked. I didn't even know if there was an office. We went to a flat that was kept especially for us in the centre of London, near Oxford Street, then "they" organized visits so that we would never meet each other. It was all for security reasons. In fact, I only knew the boys and girls with whom I trained.

I wasn't allowed to say why I was leaving and what I was doing, and nobody mentioned it. That is a big difference between the French and the English.

Are the English much stricter?

P: No. When you ask the English not to repeat something, they don't. Try asking a French person the same thing he will tell his best friend, who in turn tells his best friend and it goes on forever.

That could cause problems for an organization such as yours.

P: Definitely. But you cannot change people's natures.

Do you think it's a boastful streak in the French?

P: No. . . . I don't know. In fact I don't really understand why a French person must talk. It was one of the biggest problems between Churchill and de Gaulle. I'm sure that's why they never told de Gaulle the exact date of D-Day. They wanted to keep it a secret!

H: There were a lot of differences between France and England. I lived in both. I saw London in September 1944, in the middle of the war, and when I arrived in England, it was paradise compared to here.

Let me give you an example of the English mentality. One day we went into a department store in London. I had a ration card, I showed it—

P: No, first of all you almost fainted when you saw the displays of soap, there was such a lot of it, whereas in France we had no soap.

H: Anyway, I handed over my card, the girl took a pencil, and ticked the soap box. I didn't say a word, then I said to Pearl, "Did you see that? She used a pencil; I can rub that out in a second."

You see that's the wangling French mentality. The girl used a pencil because she was sure that people wouldn't rub it out; they had a big enough soap ration.

The English liked us all the same. Once, we were with a group of French people in a London restaurant and an English girl heard us talking in French. When we were on our way out, she turned round and shouted, "Vive la France!" It gave us a lump in our throats.

Radio Operators and Messages

Radio operators were the crucial link of communication between the SOE offices in London and the agents in France. The work of the radio operators enabled London to send orders to the agents and allowed the agents to inform London as to their needs and welfare. Because the Germans understood that these radio communications were the lifeline of the Resistance networks, they were constantly on the lookout for radio operators, making it a highly dangerous and stressful job.

P: The worst job was being a radio operator.

Why?

P: Because there were radio cars [radio detectors or "gonios"]. You had to move the radio set as often as possible so that you weren't traced, and code and decode the messages coming in and going out. It was an awful job, really stressful. Amédée did it for over a year. It was incredible that he held out in the same place for such a long time. Eventually, he asked to change jobs and became Maurice's second in command.

Amédée was born in Mauritius, but his family originated from Brittany. There were several agents from Mauritius in the SOE because they were bilingual, French-English. He lived in an apartment owned by a milliner and hid the radio set in the false bottom of an old wardrobe. One day the Germans came to the apartment. They were intrigued by the painted eggs—Amédée painted them in the Chinese way. He had learned how to do that in Mauritius.

And all the time the radio was in the wardrobe!

P: They didn't find it, but it was there all right.

Amédée was a gentleman, brought up in French bourgeois traditional fashion. The landlady thought he was an accountant working from home. One of the funniest things happened. It was after the incident of my luggage falling in the water. When it was retrieved three weeks later, Maurice took it to Amédée and asked him to dry my clothes. He hung them on lines put up in his room. He said he was very worried in case the landlady came into his room, saw my knickers drying on the line and could have thought he was having girlfriends! *(laughing)* He had such a charming way of telling that story.

The SOE radio operator near Toulouse, Yvonne Cormeau, was lucky. She lived in the countryside and could move around more easily to transmit messages. I don't know how Amédée managed for over a year in Châteauroux.

André [the son of the farmers of Doulçay, Monsieur and Madame Henri Trochet] remembered that when we were at their farm, he could see the "gonio" car driving around trying to find our radio set.

Monsieur Mardon, the mayor of Dun-le-Poëlier, first took us to Doulçay. When Amédée met him, he introduced him to Tutur, who was going to be our radio operator. We couldn't pick and choose our colleagues, we took whoever was willing. You had to trust the person who was introducing you to new contacts.

Were the radio operators technicians, people who did that professionally?

P: Most of them weren't. Mine, Tutur, was a technician because he was radio operator in the French overseas army. Amédée probably recruited him in the region of Châteauroux. He was my operator and what a character. He told such tall stories!

When he arrived at the Trochets we scattered because we thought the Gestapo was coming. He was all excited and told us how he had met Germans, shot at them and thrown hand grenades. . . . It might have been true because it was just after D-day, but all the same it was too tall a story. Listening to him I thought, Who on earth is this chap?

One of the Maquis members, Robert Knéper, caught him once, in uniform, in the middle of a tale about how the car in which he had arrived had been parachuted with him. "You see," he said, "they know how to do things properly."

He also said that his wife and children had been arrested by the Gestapo. He exaggerated so much that the people listening were in tears! Henri was a witness to that.

H: According to him, the Germans had massacred his whole family, his wife, his children . . . the chaps listening cried. In any case . . . he was a damned good operator, he knew how to do his job.

P: He became friendly with the farmers' daughters who took care of him and he decided to stay even though, for security reasons, we had to have move on. He was a danger for the Steegmans and the farm. I had to tell him off, which was a bit much because he was a professional soldier.

Also, he found decoding the messages he received boring. For a time he got other people to do it for him, even though this was forbidden for security reasons. One day one of the boys said to me, "That was an interesting message." He had decoded it himself!

H: He also got the farmers' daughters to decode messages. Tutur was never cold at night.

> *Radio messages, communicated via Morse code, were deliberately phrased in an obscure way so that the Germans wouldn't be able to easily decipher their meaning if they found them. Still, radio messages were supposed to be treated with a high level of security and destroyed after being read, but that didn't always happen: Henri kept some and shared them with M. Larroque decades later during an interview.*

"Mimi says thank you for her lovely present": to announce Pearl's arrival by parachute.

"The Marshal has swallowed his *francisc*": to announce a drop of arms. [The *francisc* was a small double-headed axe, the symbol of Marshall Pétain and the name of a decoration awarded by the Vichy government.]

H: When there were no messages left we invented them.

"Venus de Milo is knitting."

"The Victory of Samothrace is cycling."

"Rodin's *Thinker* is constipated."

Look at this coded message: the numbers are there. They started with one, two, three, four, five. When the message arrived, it was in that order. But line one for us was line 8; line 4 was line 13. The real message was revealed, but if you didn't have the code it was impossible to understand.

What language were they written in?

H: French.

Didn't the Germans manage to decode the messages?

P: They couldn't; there were two successive codes. Every radio operator had his codes printed on a silk handkerchief. They copied the sentence on top then filled in the numbers.

H: We weren't the only people sending messages. They'd have had a lot of work to do, to decode and understand thousands of messages. Even if they had managed to understand, they'd also have had to know to whom the messages were sent.

How did you know the messages were for you?

P: The messages were numbered, so I could make sure none were missing, and were addressed "To Marie."

For Marie meant it was for the Marie-Wrestler network?

H: Yes; look, this is a good message.

P: The day that one was sent I broke the "never touch intelligence work" rule. The message was so important I thought, I can't sit on this, I'll take the blame for breaking the rules. One of the intelligence networks had lost radio contact with London and had asked me to do them a favor.

H: We sent the information we had received via Paul Vannier. It concerned a trainload of petrol tanks that were on the Vierzon-Bourges line. The train was soon bombed. All 60 wagons were blown up; you could see the fire for miles. Later they sent us the following message: "Thank you for your n°47 [the number of the message]. Happy to tell you the RAF found 60 petrol wagons on the Vierzon-Bourges line, target bombed next morning with good results. Supreme commander asks us to congratulate you for all information sent in 47." In other words, all the information we had sent.

It was headquarters congratulating us because the petrol in those 60 wagons was destined to move German troops to Normandy. They couldn't leave and were blocked in the region for at least a week.

H: Let me show you some of the radio messages.

P: We shouldn't have those.

Didn't he tell you he had kept those messages?

P: No.

Where did you hide them?

P: I don't know where he hid them, but you can see what a state they're in.

Who kept them, you?

H: Tutur, the radio operator.

P: It wasn't Tutur, it was you.

H: No it wasn't.

P: I received the decoded messages from Tutur and I didn't return them to him. You kept them.

H: Do you think I'd ever do such a thing as that?

P: Well then . . . (*Henri laughs*)

You don't seem to be sure about it.

H: I can't remember if I kept them or not. I'd be surprised if I had, seeing as I'm so disciplined.

P: Oh no. It just isn't true. *(laughter)*

H: [Reading messages aloud] "Quasimodo is a fête," "Don't play about in the morning," "Sherry is a Spanish wine," "A badly dressed woman." These four messages meant "Intensify guerrilla warfare," "Cut telephone communications," "Block the roads," and "Sabotage railway lines."

P: These four messages arrived just before D-Day; they were sent on the evening of June 5.

H: After receiving one, Robert Knéper and I spent all night outside cutting telephone lines. At the same time, other lads were felling trees across the road in La Taille de Ruine. Then there was this one, completely incredible, sometimes London didn't have a clue about our work in France. "For Marie: can you tell us where the 11th Armoured Division is, we think it is in your region Stop. Tell us how many bogies there are on each tank in your region, as well as the distinguishing marks and indications concerning the division."

Why didn't they ask us to get hold of a tank and send it in spare parts while they were at it? They didn't realize the danger for us; you have to stick your head under a tank to know how many bogies there are—assuming you knew what a bogie was. I didn't know. Where are bogies?

P: Bogies are wheels inside the traction band.

H: You have to get very close to be able to count them.

P: Or to see soldiers' distinguishing badges.

H: Yes. "Excuse me sir, where are you from, can I see your badge please?" There were some far-fetched messages.

Pearl's Personality

Do you think that during the war you had to set yourself certain challenges, do extraordinary things, counting only on yourself?

P: Partly, but I don't consider I did anything extraordinary. Even today when people say, "You know, you did some incredible things, they weren't easy," I still don't believe it's true. I did it because I wanted to, because it was useful, because it had to be done.

Did you want to prove something?

P: To myself, yes, because I was very shy and always suffered because of it.

It's hard to believe you were shy.

P: I still am. But whereas Henri is shy with individual people, I'm shy in a group. With one person, I'm not shy at all. But I hate being in meetings, or receptions, or going into cafés or restaurants on my own. Even now I don't like it.

Do you think it is shyness or just reticence about certain types of human relationships, in public?

P: I don't know what it is, I'm paralyzed.

So you don't feel at ease, but you're not really frightened?

P: Yes, I'm frightened of groups.

H: Yet for some time now you have been making speeches to groups of people.

P: But can you remember when I first had to do it? Even though it was in front of people I knew, it was dreadful. You can't imagine what I went through.

H: Yes, I'm sure it wasn't easy.

P: Now it's easier for me, because . . .

Because you have slowly gotten used to it.

P: No. I'm still not used to it. On June 12, 1994, [at the inauguration of the Les Souches monument at La Chapelle-Montmartin
in the Loir-et-Cher], I didn't want to prepare a written speech,
but when I was there I didn't say half the things I'd planned
because I just couldn't. First I have to make a big effort to control myself, to push all my problems back inside, before I can say
anything.

Maybe these events bring back bad memories?
H: Yes.

*(It's tea-time. Pauline points out her "jumbo cup" saying she only takes
one cup of tea, when in fact it's equal to at least three.)*

P: There, I have an elephant cup. Do you know my mother
always called me "the elephant" when I was little; she would
always say "you great big elephant."

H: But you weren't fat.

P: No, but I was the eldest child and I was taller than the others.
I was always fairly tall. But, in fact I am like an elephant; I have
the memory of an elephant. I'm also slightly, what shall I say,
clumsy. I'm not very dexterous.

And when you go forward . . .

P: I go straight forward, like an elephant. I have always been
fairly slow, except for packing: I can pack a suitcase in no time; I
did it so often during the clandestine period.

At the outset I'm not someone who criticizes people or things automatically, I tend to criticize later. It is an attitude that has caused me to be disappointed several times in life. If I like someone very much, I put them on a pedestal. Then one fine day they fall off and I'm horribly disappointed. It's my own fault; I shouldn't put people on pedestals because human beings are what they are. They have good as well as not so good sides to their characters. To start with I only see the good side, and sometimes it can last for a long time.

Do you think one can foresee things clearly?

P: No. Maybe it's part of being British; if I give my affection to someone, I give wholly. I don't hold anything back. Then if all of a sudden the person lets me down, I have difficulty forgetting. But I don't hold it against them, it's finished. Amen.

When I started working for the Resistance, I threw myself into it as I would have done with a friend whom I love. When I say "love" it isn't anything physical, it's completely psychological. I threw myself into the work because I wanted to do it and I enjoyed doing it. I build psychological, not physical, relationships with people. I have had some very, very good friends, I mean real friends—both male and female—but that's all. There are people I liked enormously, for example my boss before the war, Douglas Colyer. He was an extraordinary person, very humane, very warm, and very understanding. One day I said to an officer who knew him that I liked Dougie a lot. He replied, "Yes, well, he is very attractive."

"That's not what I mean." I could have hit him.

While I was with all those men in the Maquis, there was never anything between us. Obviously there were times in the course of my life when some of the chaps made a pass. But pals are pals; that's all. Someone said to me recently after seeing a photograph of me when I was young—the photo had been set up in a studio, I wasn't as pretty as that—"Well, I'm not surprised so many men followed you."

H: You are always demeaning yourself physically: "I wasn't as pretty as that." Yes you were, you were like that.

P: I could have hit him as well. I don't like such comments. Why does everything have to be centered around that subject? Something that really annoys me today is that physical aspects are all-important. What has happened to feelings? In my opinion it's a disaster.

How did you put up with the stress and anxiety during the clandestine period? . . . It could have gone wrong at any time.

P: Well I have a very British character. I knew that I had to pay attention. But I'm sensitive to everything around me, I think it helped to keep me going for so long. I've always had my antennae turned on, but particularly at that time.

Could you tell when there was danger?

P: I could feel it. It didn't stop me having two or three horrifying frights, but I didn't live in a state of permanent anxiety. It was a bit stressful because we had to keep on the move, we didn't use telephones, we didn't write, we traveled mostly by train—usually at night. We didn't sleep very much and it was extremely solitary work. We never knew if we were going to be arrested and interrogated, or if Germans were going to be waiting for us when we went into a house.

At the time I do not remember being very anxious, but it marked me all the same. I felt it for a long time afterward. Eight years after the liberation of France, I was walking in the Trocadéro gardens and I nearly fainted, which is something I never do. I was with my young daughter, one Sunday afternoon. She said something to me. I bent down toward her, stood up, and found myself facing three Germans in uniform. What a shock, my daughter still remembers it today.

Have you ever inexplicably felt danger and trusted your intuition?

P: No. The only time I woke up in the middle of the night was when I dreamed about policemen. It happened twice, once the night before Maurice Southgate was arrested and once the night before June 11 [the Battle of Les Souches]. But I can't say I have any intuition about what is going to happen, like a clairvoyant for instance.

Do you believe some people have a sixth sense when they are facing danger?

P: Yes. Philippe de Vomécourt ["Saint Paul"] was like that. One day he told me a story that really struck me. During the war he was with someone in a hotel. He woke up in the middle of the night and he went to wake up the other agent, saying, "We have to leave immediately, do you hear?"

"No, I don't want to, I'm staying here."

"It's an order, get out."

A few hours later the police raided the hotel. He could feel it was going to happen.

He spent many years in Africa. He told of things that happened there that make your hair stand on end. There were cases of people arriving by car at a village, who couldn't enter because the villagers didn't want them. They just couldn't move, impossible, even though there was no one there; just was an invisible wall. He once gave a message to a man who set off to walk through a deep forest and one hour later the same man

handed over the message 30 km away. There's no doubt about
it, it exists.

*Do you think the culture or sensitivity he developed in that environ-
ment was useful to him during the war?*

P: Definitely. How can it be explained, it is so intangible. Waves
exist that we cannot control, that's the mystery.

Philosophy and Religion

P: I believe in destiny.

What do you mean by that?

P: There's no doubt about it, your destiny is written, mapped
out—call it what you like. There are certain things you have
to face. They may come when you are young, middle-aged, or
elderly. If you really observe people around you, you ask yourself, "Why is it they lead such a life?"

My cousin, the one whose mother sent me her old clothes,
said to me one day, "I never understood why you weren't jealous of me."

"Why should I be jealous of you?"

"Because things were so much easier for me than they ever
were for you."

"No, I wasn't jealous. Quite the opposite, I benefited by it."

She always had an easy life, until one day, because her husband and her mother had both died, she suddenly found herself
alone. She was completely lost because everything had been so
easy for her. I believe your destiny is mapped out when you set
off in life. If you know how to steer it, you may be able to direct
it slightly, but not always and never completely.

Do you think you are born with a plan for your life?

P: I'm sure of it.

There are ordeals to get through, things to take advantage of, help that may come your way.

P: Unfortunately, we don't know what they are from the start, but it's certain they are there.

H: You're talking about destiny, but that's another unfair thing in life. Because there are great destinies, and then people who have bad ones.

P: Some people have dreadful destinies that improve. Others begin well, then, in the middle, things go wrong and it is back to square one. It is a movement, a tide that ebbs and flows. What can help you? That is the mystery.

I was brought up as a Protestant. There was no question of missing church on a Sunday. Just we four girls went. Mummy never accompanied us, probably because she had hearing problems. We went to church but we weren't christened, that was something to do with my father again.

When I was 16 the only person I could confide in was the vicar. Mummy must have seen him on several occasions about our financial problems. One day I went to see him, to talk to him about my troubles with Mummy; I needed his advice. He must have thought I was coming about money problems because he hadn't time to see me.

I took it very badly. I thought, If I cannot find help in religion, who else is going to help me? It was a turning point for me. I didn't want anything to do with religion until I met Henri. He, too, was raised a Protestant. The question was brought out in the open again. Henri gave me lectures, saying it wasn't possible to go through life without a religion.

When I arrived in England in 1941, I thought maybe Henri was right. I was staying at the Young Women's Christian Association in London. The matron told me that a minister came every Tuesday evening to talk about religion and if I was interested I would be welcome. I said I would go if I didn't leave work too late.

My sisters and I were christened in 1939. My mind opened to religious questions, and one day when the minister told me I ought to make my confession [in the Anglican church], I replied, "What, me? It's out of the question."

"You can make your confession to someone else; you don't have to do it with me."

"That's not the point. The person to whom I confess may have done something worse than me. I don't agree with that."

If I have done something wrong, I punish myself; I take care of the consequences. But I don't need to be punished by someone else. After that, he started talking about eternal life, but I told him I didn't believe in it. He was rather taken aback and very troubled by my lack of belief.

"Would you convince someone else that there is no life after death?" he continued.

"Not at all. One is free to believe whatever one chooses."

All this is just to explain that I am a believer but I don't practice. I go to church on my own, where I want and also where I can find one open. I would be very happy to discuss religion one day with a theologian. But for me, religion is something really personal. Apparently that's not how it should be perceived. It should be viewed collectively as something universal.

The basis of religion is, as far as I'm concerned, the Ten Commandments. After that, I don't see. . . .

But do you not think that meditating in a church is something beyond the Ten Commandments?

P: To whatever or whomever one is addressing, whether it's Christ—I think I prefer to address God directly—we had to create an image of him, because otherwise people wouldn't understand, but as far as I am concerned, he is a spirit. There is no doubt about it, we are surrounded by something.

Human beings need something to cling on to. You have it, for instance, when you are a Christian and you go to church. When you stop going, how do you replace it? The physical, material part has nothing to do with what you feel in aspiring to do something, deep inside you, to help give you the moral strength to cope with life's difficulties.

You may say you can always have a drink, then a second, then a third, that's a very easy thing to do! From the moment I realized that my father was an alcoholic, with all the misery it brought us, I swore to myself I would never drink. When first I met Henri, I warned him I would never accept it if he started drinking.

Have you ever thought that although you did not have a good father, it wasn't altogether by chance? That somehow it prepared you and helped you succeed during this important period of your life when you were working for the Resistance? Don't you see some sort of meaning in all that?

P: Definitely.

Do you think that during difficult times we find things to support us?

P: Yes, I'm sure of it. But I'm glad to have done what I did, rather than starting life now. I feel sorry for youngsters today.

Why?

P: Because we haven't given them the means to defend themselves. Life when you are an adult always holds problems in store and you need self-discipline to cope with them. We no longer teach children they need discipline.

Children are undisciplined. Listen, the other day I was in the metro, but I felt as if I were in a cage full of monkeys. They don't have any respect for anyone. They push and shove to get in the carriage, they talk loudly, laugh at you, they even say rude words—it is madness. It is mostly the parents' fault. If you don't have any discipline in your life, how can you expect to manage? You cannot solve a problem for yourself if all your life you have been told "yes" and "amen" to every request you have made.

For discipline you had no choice, you absolutely had to—

P: Mummy told me to do something, I did it. I never questioned it.

But you realized that if you didn't solve some of the family's problems, the whole family ran the risk of a catastrophe.

P: Maybe.

If the worst came to the worst you could have ended up in an orphanage or somewhere similar.

P: I didn't think about orphanages because I didn't know what they were. If we pulled through as well as we did, it was thanks to my mother, because she did cope, even if she did have some help from me. I started to work to meet my family's needs. It was common in those days. Henri started working for his father for nothing; André Trochet worked for his father without being paid.

Let me tell you something strange that happened when I was trying to change jobs, I mean when I wanted to join SOE. I had a colleague in the Air Ministry who virtually lived with clairvoyants—she spent her lunch hours visiting them. She would come back saying that I absolutely had to go to see one or the other. My first reaction was to ask how much. She would tell me the price and I always replied it was too expensive; I'd rather go to the cinema.

One day she came back saying the clairvoyant she had seen was sensational. I asked her how much and she said it was two shillings and six pence, so I said I would go. It was to keep her quiet more than anything else. At lunchtime we both went to see the clairvoyant.

She was in Oxford Street in a sort of amusement arcade. She was in a small hut and she looked into a crystal ball. I'd never experienced that. First she gave me the "virgin" ball and she made me hold it for a while. Then without touching it, she put it in a purple handkerchief. She turned the ball round and told me all about my past life, but in every little detail! I was a very taken aback. She continued, then suddenly, with urgency she said, "You want to change jobs. What do you want to do?"

"I want to change jobs; that's all I can say."

"Give me your hand."

I gave her my hand and she said, "You will get through it all right."

I asked her for information about Henri, because I didn't know exactly where he was but she couldn't say anything about him. Finally, at the end of the séance, she announced, "At the end of the war, you will go to the United States."

I thought she was completely mad; I could see no reason why I should go to the States. I went to see the clairvoyant believing and disbelieving at the same time, and yet really I did pull through and did go to the States.

H: In any case, she couldn't very well say "you will not come through it."

P: She *knew* that it was dangerous. She didn't tell me that, but she made me sense it. I was in the midst of talks about joining the SOE . . .

Did that make an impression on you, did it encourage you?

P: It comforted me. I told myself it may be true or may not be true, I didn't know. I cannot say that I do not believe at all, because there is something there. Against all logic, there is something. But I'm incapable of saying what, exactly. I'm not saying I've never been to a séance, but I'm very wary of it because I know it's dangerous. But there is something there, no doubt about it.

NOTES

Introduction

39 of them were women: Although different sources quote different numbers, the detail-oriented Vera Atkins, second in command to the head of the F Section, told SOE author Rita Kramer that 39 women trained by the SOE were sent into France.

Chapter 1: A Difficult Childhood

last male descendant of Sir Richard Witherington: M. R. D. Foot, preface to the unpublished English translation of *Pauline.*

Chapter 3: Escape from France

between six to eight million French: The Fall of France, 174.

Chapter 4: Training and Preparation in the Ranks of the SOE

Pearl, along with 14 others . . . (number of WAAFs in the SOE): *The Heroines of the SOE,* 13.

. . . cool and resourceful . . .
. . . plenty of intelligence . . .
. . . probably the best shot . . .
. . . sound knowledge of weapons . . .
. . . very capable . . .
All remarks from Pearl's SOE instructors are taken from #42 of
Pearl's SOE files.

would give us some protection: According to the Geneva Conventions, a set of international rules regarding warfare established
in 1929, and the Hague Convention of Land Warfare of 1907,
an enemy combatant captured during a time of war was to be
imprisoned humanely. But after France's surrender to Germany,
a state of war did not exist between those two countries and so
anyone appearing to be a civilian caught fighting against the
occupying force would be judged according to the country's
current laws, not according to the Geneva or Hague Conventions. Women were not even considered combatants so the SOE
women were in great danger of being shot if captured.

Chapter 5: Parachuting into Occupied France

Maurice Southgate sent Henri: Behind Enemy Lines, 69.

Chapter 6: Courier Missions, Code Names, and Covers

Pearl's courier worked overlapped: That the SOE had intended
Pearl for both courier and liaison work before they sent her in
can be found in her SOE files #31, #34.

Chapter 7: The Michelin Factory Affair

some of them begrudgingly: The Michelin family worked with the
Germans somewhat begrudgingly—the head of the company
was referred to by the German authorities as "the taciturn

one"—and their wartime production output was far below that of their prewar output, possibly deliberately. Because of this—but more because certain members of the Michelin family were willing to support the Allied cause during the war (as Pearl notes in this chapter, a member of the Michelin family living in London told the RAF how to precisely bomb the factory)—the collaboration of the Michelin family was overlooked after the liberation. *Les hommes du pneu: Les ouvriers Michelin a Clermont-Ferrand de 1940 a 1980* (Collection Movements Social) (French edition). For an English book covering similar material, see *The Michelin Men: Driving an Empire* by Herbert R. Lottman.

Chapter 8: Arrest of a Resistance Leader

Maurice Southgate had sent a note: Behind Enemy Lines, 94.

When he opened the door: Behind Enemy Lines, 94

a huge pile of cash: Paul McCue states the amount as one million francs (*Behind Enemy Lines*, 94).

He asked him if he could get us out of town: The circuitous and lengthy route taken by Pearl and Henri out of Montlucon and then back into the same area was designed to throw any possible pursuers off their track. Conversation with H. Larroque.

Chapter 9: The Battle of Les Souches

So the Germans kept the four women: The account of what happened inside the house with the four women was later written down by Yvonne Sebassier and provided to Pearl.

Chapter 10: Organizing the Maquis

Pearl's image was placed on "wanted" posters: SOE in France, 335. M. R. D. Foot mentions that at this point, Pearl's image was placed on multiple posters by the Germans offering a one-million-franc reward for her capture. No copy of this poster exists, nor is there any eyewitness description of its contents. Foot cites a 1946 book, *Maquis S.S.4* by Michael Mockers, one of Peal's subsector leaders, as his source for this information. However, Mockers only says it was a large reward, without stating the amount, and suggests that the posters were limited to Montlucon. Pearl never mentioned the posters to M. Larroque during their interviews, or in the detailed reports that she submitted to the SOE at the end of her service, and in 2007 she told another journalist that their existence was never proven. Despite all of this doubt, it is still generally believed that the reward posters did exist.

which she renamed Marie-Wrestler circuit: Why Pearl named her section of the Stationer network "Marie-Wrestler" is taken from her SOE files #25 and #29.

Pearl had expressed alarm: Pearl's SOE file #34 reveals her alarm at liaising with a 1,000-man-strong Maquis group.

Pearl provided information . . . See Appendix titled "Radio Messages."

we had about 500,000 francs: This was an enormous amount of money. To give an idea exactly how enormous, in 1944, the franc was worth about 90 cents. Average yearly wages in America at the same time would have been about $2,400; a typical house would have cost about $3,500, and a new car would have cost about $1,000 if you would have been able to purchase one. (The auto factories had stopped making new cars in order to produce war materials such as planes and tanks, so it would have been almost impossible to purchase a new car during the war.)

Chapter 11: Into the Forest

The captain called over to them: This incident shows how much control the Nazis exercised over their men. Even though the condemned captain was about to be killed, the German prisoners walking past still stopped, saluted him, and meekly accepted his verbal abuse. The Alsatian (from German-occupied Alsace) who had deserted, on the other hand, felt no such loyalty, was most likely fed up with the false moral superiority of the Nazi regime, and so had no trouble permanently silencing the haranguing German captain. Although what the captain was saying to the other Germans isn't specifically mentioned, it's very likely that he was criticizing their acceptance of prisoner status instead of insisting on execution like he had.

a column of 18,000 Germans: This was a diverse group of German survivors—Luftwafe, Marine, Heer—under the command of Colonel Eric Elster that started from the Bay of Biscay and moved northeast to try to get back to Germany.

a mission of the Gaullist regional military: Relations between the British government and General Charles de Gaulle were so strained that when he marched into Paris in August 1944, de Gaulle gave speeches that implied that France had liberated itself without any outside help. He was not even terribly polite to French Resistance leaders, especially the Communists—whom he saw as a dangerous political threat—and even less so to British SOE agents, most of whom he gave just 48 hours notice to get out of France.

Chapter 12: Postwar Life

Vera Atkins received authorization: Vera Atkins: A Life in Secrets, 212ff.

I jumped, I went into operation; I was going to wear them: If Pearl hadn't received the parachute wings how could she have worn them? It wasn't difficult to get hold of them in postwar France so apparently Pearl obtained some unofficial wings and wore them when the occasion called for it. But she was finally granted official parachute wings by a senior RAF parachute instructor in 2006.

Also not mentioned in the narrative, because it occurred after the Larroque interviews, was that Pearl was awarded with the CBE—Commander of the Most Excellent Order of the British Empire—in 2004 by Queen Elizabeth.

We've lost everything: Henri described his immediate postwar employment during an interview with Hervé Larroque (not included in this book) as "the winding up of American surplus stocks, medical and surgical equipment." Henri went on to say that "one of my friends, Jacques Bureau, found me the job. He was in charge of winding up this unit. I remained there until the business closed down; it fizzled out gradually when all the stocks were liquidated. There were only three of us left [at the end]." Since this was obviously going to be temporary employment, in a way it seems odd that Henri would be surprised that his work there had suddenly "gone bust," as Pearl describes it (unless it fizzled out much quicker than he had originally been led to believe). It is possible that this was instead referring to his parents' beauty salon (where Henri had worked from 1926 to 1930) or the cleaning-product business he started in 1938 (see page 133), but as Pearl and Henri did not provide enough specific information in their interviews about the postwar running of these businesses, this is pure speculation.

One of the biggest mysteries: Although there is no doubt that Déricourt was directly responsible for the arrest (and subsequent death) of many agents of the Prosper network, despite having been brought to trial several times he always went free. It is believed by many people that someone in the British government, higher than the SOE, kept him from justice because he knew too much. For more on Déricourt, see the following: *Flames in the Field*, 210–22; *Vera Atkins: A Life in Secrets*, 356–64; *SOE in France*, throughout but especially 259–67; and *Déricourt: The Chequered Spy.*

BIBLIOGRAPHY

Basu, Shrabani. *Spy Princess: The Life of Noor Inayat Khan*. New York: Omega Publications, 2006.

Chambard, Claude. *The Maquis: A History of the French Resistance Movement*. Translated by Elaine P. Halperin. New York: The Bobbs-Merrill Company, Inc., 1976.

Churchill, Winston S., ed. *Never Give In! The Best of Winston Churchill's Speeches*. Great Britain: Pimlico, 2003.

Crowdy, Terry and Steve Noon (illustrator). *French Resistance Fighter: France's Secret Army*. Great Britain: Osprey Publishing, Ltd., 2007.

Dildy, Douglas C. and Howard Gerrard (illustrator). *Dunkirk 1940: Operation Dynamo*. Great Britain: Osprey Publishing, Ltd., 2010.

Escott, Beryl E. *The Heroines of the SOE F Section: Britain's Secret Women in France*. Great Britain: The History Press, 2010.

Foot, M. R. D. *SOE in France. An Account of the Work of the British Special Operations Executive in France 1940–1944*. London: HSMO, 1966.

Gueslin, Andre, ed. *Les hommes du pneu: Les ouvriers Michelin a Clermont-Ferrand de 1940 a 1980.* Collection Movements Social.

Helm, Sarah. *A Life in Secrets: Vera Atkins and the Missing Agents of WWII.* New York: Doubleday, 2005.

Jackson, Julian. *The Fall of France: The Nazi Invasion of 1940.* Oxford: Oxford University Press, 2003.

Jackson, Julian. *France: The Dark Years 1940–1944.* Oxford: Oxford University Press, 2001.

Kramer, Rita. *Flames in the Field: The Story of Four SOE Agents in Occupied France.* London: Michael Joseph, 1995.

Lottman, Herbert R. *The Michelin Men: Driving an Empire.* London/New York: I.B. Tauris & Co.,Ltd., 2003.

McCue, Paul. *Behind Enemy Lines with the SAS: The Story of Amédée Maingard—SOE Agent.* Great Britain: Pen & Sword, Ltd., 2007.

Overton Fuller, Jean. *Déricourt: The Chequered Spy.* Wilton, UK: Michael Russell, 1989.

Overton Fuller, Jean. *Madeleine.* London: Golliancz, 1952.

Pattinson, Juliette. *Gender, Passing, and the Special Operations Executive in the Second World War.* Manchester, UK: Manchester University Press, 2006.

Riding, Alan. *And the Show Went On: Cultural Life in Nazi-Occupied Paris.* New York: Alfred A. Knopf, 2010.

SOE Personnel Files. The National Archives. www.National Archives.gov.uk.

Starns, Penny. *Odette: World War Two's Darling Spy.* Stroud, UK: The History Press, 2009.

Wake, Nancy. *The Autobiography of the Woman the Gestapo Called the White Mouse.* Sydney: Sun Books, 1985.

INDEX